ASIAN AMERICAN FOLKTALES

ASIAN AMERICAN FOLKTALES

Edited by
Thomas A. Green

Stories from the American Mosaic

GREENWOOD PRESS
Westport, Connecticut • London

Library of Congress Cataloging-in-Publication Data

Asian American folktales / edited by Thomas A. Green.
    p. cm. – (Stories from the American mosaic)
Includes bibliographical references and index.
ISBN 978-0-313-36297-2 (alk. paper)
1. Asian Americans–Folklore. 2. Tales–United States. 3. Tales–Asia. I. Green, Thomas A.,
1944-
GR111.A75   2009
398.2'08995073–dc22   2008047454

British Library Cataloguing in Publication Data is available.

Library of Congress Catalog Card Number: 2008047454
ISBN: 978-0-313-36297-2

First published in 2009

Greenwood Press, 88 Post Road West, Westport, CT 06881
An imprint of Greenwood Publishing Group, Inc.
www.greenwood.com

Printed in the United States of America

The paper used in this book complies with the
Permanent Paper Standard issued by the National
Information Standards Organization (Z39.48-1984).

10 9 8 7 6 5 4 3 2 1

Contents

Preface

Asian American Folktales is designed to provide educators, students, and general readers with examples of a range of traditional Asian American narrative types: fictional tales, legends, myths, and personal experience narratives. This collection cannot hope to represent the vast range of Asian cultural traditions in the United States. Therefore, examples have been selected from South Asia (India), Southeast Asia (The Philippines), and East Asia (China, Japan, and Korea) folktale repertoires. The selection of these groups is not intended to reflect population statistics or historical significance. Rather, these cultures are well-established in the contemporary United States, and extensive collections of each group's folktales have been translated into English.

The Chinese presence began to develop in the mid-nineteenth century with laborers (primarily single males) coming to work most notably on the railroads, but also in the mining industry and other occupations. Between the passage of the Chinese Exclusion Act of 1882 and its repeal in 1943, the Chinese American population decreased dramatically, but was revitalized during the latter half of the twentieth century.

American Japanese communities that began to develop, primarily on the West Coast in the late-nineteenth century experienced a similar setback in 1908 as a result of the Root-Takahira Agreement. Popularly known as the "Gentlemen's Agreement," it called for the voluntary restriction of Japanese emigration to the United States. Nevertheless, Japanese Americans began to put down roots until the initiation of armed conflict between Japan and the United States in 1941 and the subsequent internment of many Americans of Japanese descent. Ironically, for many the relocation experience ultimately revitalized rather than eradicated Asian identity and traditional culture.

Although immigration quotas established in the 1920s impacted all Asian immigration until the elimination of this system in 1984, South Asian, Filipino, and Korean populations were not affected as dramatically as were the Chinese and Japanese. American descendants of each of these groups maintain a significant presence in the twenty-first century.

The tales preserved within each of the groups reflect religious practices (for example, "The Princess Kwan-yin," pp. 3–8), folk beliefs (as in "The

Fearless Captain," pp. 143–44), ethical principles (for example, "The Quarrel of the Monkey and the Crab," pp. 108–13), stock characters (see "Juan Pusong," pp. 74–76), and other prevailing concerns of the respective Asian traditions from which they are drawn. In many instances, tales from Asian, as distinct from Asian American, collections were included in the interest of including more fully developed narrative texts. In such cases, the existence of these tales in the respective Asian American repertoires was verified through published sources or resource persons of Asian descent. The introductions to each tale comment on these issues. The concluding general bibliography provides additional resources for those readers who wish to explore Asian American traditions in greater depth.

The collection is divided into four sections. "Origins" encompasses those narratives that focus on beginnings and transformations: the creation of the world and its inhabitants, how animal species acquired their physical characteristics, and how the family came to be here, for example. "Heroes, Heroines, Tricksters, and Fools" presents a cross-section of major character types that populate Asian American folktales. "Society and Conflict" contains considerations of social issues ranging from conventional morality to intergroup conflicts. Finally, "The Supernatural" concentrates on traditional tales of the dead, the magical, and the monstrous.

Some of the narratives have been modified from their original forms for the benefit of contemporary readers. The modifications have been held to the minimum necessary to translate these tales for their intended audiences and to eliminate redundancy in some cases. In a few cases, alternative terminology has been substituted for terms (particularly racially charged terms) that would prove offensive to contemporary readers. The source of each selection is noted at its conclusion for the benefit of readers who wish to read the original texts.

My thanks go out to Richa Dhanju, Sam Mannan, and Suhani Patel who generously contributed their time and advice during the South Asian text selection process.

ORIGINS

The Princess Kwan-yin

The goddess Kwan-yin (or Guan-yin) is revered in traditional Chinese and Chinese American culture as the embodiment of compassion. Recognized by both Daoists and Buddhists, the following narrative is a variant of the most well-known myth of her early trials and canonization. Her images often portray her atop a dragon, or she may be accompanied by a tiger. In either case, she may be holding a vase of pure water. All of these features allude to episodes in the tale of "The Princess Kwan-yin." Singer-composer Alanis Morissette, in her "Citizen of the Planet" (2008), refers to the goddess Kwan-yin.

Once upon a time in China there lived a certain king who had three daughters. The fairest and best of these was Kwan-yin, the youngest. The old king was justly proud of this daughter, for of all the women who had ever lived in the palace she was by far the most attractive. It did not take him long, therefore, to decide that she should be the heir to his throne, and her husband ruler of his kingdom. But, strange to say, Kwan-yin was not pleased at this good fortune. She cared little for the pomp and splendor of court life. She foresaw no pleasure for herself in ruling as a queen, but even feared that in so high a station she might feel out of place and unhappy.

Every day she went to her room to read and study. As a result of this daily labor she soon went far beyond her sisters along the paths of knowledge, and her name was known in the farthest corner of the kingdom as "Kwan-yin, the wise princess." Besides being very fond of books, Kwan-yin was thoughtful of her friends. She was careful about her behavior both in public and in private. Her warm heart was open at all times to the cries of those in trouble.

She was kind to the poor and suffering. She won the love of the lower classes, and was to them a sort of goddess to whom they could appeal whenever they were hungry and in need. Some people even believed that she was a fairy who had come to earth from her home within the Western Heaven, while others said that once, long years before, she had lived in the world as a prince instead of a princess. However this may be, one thing is certain Kwan-yin was pure and good, and well deserved the praises that were showered upon her.

One day the king called this favorite daughter to the royal bedside, for he felt that the hour of death was drawing near. Kwan-yin kowtowed before her royal father, kneeling and touching her forehead on the floor in sign of deepest reverence. The old man bade her rise and come closer. Taking her hand tenderly in his own, he said, "Daughter, you know well how I love you. Your modesty and virtue, your talent and your love of knowledge, have made you first in my heart. As you know already, I chose you as heir to my kingdom long ago. I promised that your husband should be made ruler in my stead. The time is almost ripe for me to ascend upon the dragon and become a guest on high. It is necessary that you be given at once in marriage."

"But, most exalted father," faltered the princess, "I am not ready to be married."

"Not ready, child! Why, are you not eighteen? Are not the daughters of our nation often wedded long before they reach that age? Because of your desire for learning I have spared you thus far from any thought of a husband, but now we can wait no longer."

"Royal father, hear your child, and do not compel her to give up her dearest pleasures. Let her go into a quiet convent where she may lead a life of study!"

The king sighed deeply at hearing these words. He loved his daughter and did not wish to wound her. "Kwan-yin," he continued, "do you wish to pass by the green spring of youth, to live up this mighty kingdom? Do you wish to enter the doors of a convent where women say farewell to life and all its pleasures? No! Your father will not permit this. It grieves me sorely to disappoint you, but one month from this very day you shall be married. I have chosen for your royal partner a man of many noble parts. You know him by name already, although you have not seen him. Remember that, of the hundred virtues filial conduct is the chief, and that you owe more to me than to all else on earth."

Kwan-yin turned pale. Trembling, she would have sunk to the floor, but her mother and sisters supported her, and by their tender care brought her back to consciousness.

Every day of the month that followed, Kwan-yin's relatives begged her to give up what they called her foolish notion. Her sisters had long since given up hope of becoming queen. They were amazed at her stupidity. The very thought of any one's choosing a convent instead of a throne was to them a sure sign of madness. Over and over again they asked her reason for making so strange a choice. To every question, she shook her head, replying, "A voice from the heavens speaks to me, and I must obey it."

On the eve of the wedding day Kwan-yin slipped out of the palace, and, after a weary journey, arrived at a convent called, "The Cloister of the White Sparrow." She was dressed as a poor maiden. She said she wished to become a nun. The abbess, not knowing who she was, did not receive her kindly. Indeed, she told Kwan-yin that they could not receive her into the sisterhood, that the building was full. Finally, after Kwan-yin had shed many tears, the abbess let her enter, but only as a sort of servant, who might be cast out for the slightest fault.

Now that Kwan-yin found herself in the life which she had long dreamt of leading, she tried to be satisfied. But the nuns seemed to wish to make her stay among them most miserable. They gave her the hardest tasks to do, and it was seldom that she had a minute to rest. All day long she was busy, carrying water from a well at the foot of the convent hill or gathering wood from a neighboring forest. At night when her back was almost breaking, she was given many extra tasks, enough to have crushed the spirit of any other woman than this brave daughter of a king. Forgetting her grief, and trying to hide the lines of pain that sometimes wrinkled her fair forehead, she tried to make these hard-hearted women love her. In return for their rough words, she spoke to them kindly, and never did she give way to anger.

One day while poor Kwan-yin was picking up brushwood in the forest she heard a tiger making his way through the bushes. Having no means of defending herself, she breathed a silent prayer to the gods for help, and calmly awaited the coming of the great beast.

To her surprise, when the bloodthirsty animal appeared, instead of bounding up to tear her in pieces, he began to make a soft purring noise. He did not try to hurt Kwan-yin, but rubbed against her in a friendly manner, and let her pat him on the head.

The next day the princess went back to the same spot. There she found no fewer than a dozen savage beasts working under the command of the friendly tiger, gathering wood for her. In a short time enough brush and fire-wood had been piled up to last the convent for six months. Thus, even the wild animals of the forest were better able to judge of her goodness than the women of the sisterhood.

At another time when Kwan-yin was toiling up the hill for the twentieth time, carrying two great pails of water on a pole, an enormous dragon faced her in the road. Now, in China, the dragon is sacred, and Kwan-yin was not at all frightened, for she knew that she had done no wrong.

The animal looked at her for a moment, switched its horrid tail, and shot out fire from its nostrils. Then, dashing the burden from the startled maiden's shoulder, it vanished. Full of fear, Kwan-yin hurried up the hill to the nunnery. As she drew near the inner court, she was amazed to see in the center of the open space a new building of solid stone. It had sprung up by magic since her last journey down the hill. On going forward, she saw that there were four arched doorways to the fairy house. Above the door facing west was a tablet with these words written on it: "In honor of Kwan-yin, the faithful princess." Inside was a well of the purest water, while, for drawing this water, there was a strange machine, the like of which neither Kwan-yin nor the nuns had ever seen.

The sisters knew that this magic well was a monument to Kwan-yin's goodness. For a few days they treated her much better. "Since the gods have dug a well at our very gate," they said, "this girl will no longer need to bear water from the foot of the hill. For what strange reason, however, did the gods write this beggar's name on the stone?"

Kwan-yin heard their unkind remarks in silence. She could have explained the meaning of the dragon's gift, but she chose to let her companions remain in ignorance. At last the selfish nuns began to grow careless again, and treated her even worse than before. They could not bear to see the poor girl enjoy a moment's idleness.

"This is a place for work," they told her. "All of us have labored hard to win our present station. You must do likewise." So they robbed her of every chance for study and prayer, and gave her no credit for the magic well.

One night the sisters were awakened from their sleep by strange noises, and soon they heard outside the walls of the compound the blare of a trumpet. A great army had been sent by Kwan-yin's father to attack the convent, for his spies had at last been able to trace the runaway princess to this holy retreat.

"Oh, who has brought this woe upon us?" exclaimed all the women, looking at each other in great fear. "Who has done this great evil? There is one among us who has sinned most terribly, and now the gods are about to destroy us." They gazed at one another, but no one thought of Kwan-yin, for they did not believe her of enough importance to attract the anger of heaven, even though she might have done the most shocking of deeds. Then, too, she had been so meek and lowly while in their holy order that they did not once dream of charging her with any crime.

The threatening sounds outside grew louder and louder. All at once a fearful cry arose among the women: "They are about to burn our sacred dwelling." Smoke was rising just beyond the enclosure where the soldiers were kindling a great fire, the heat of which would soon be great enough to make the convent walls crumble into dust.

Suddenly a voice was heard above the tumult of the weeping sisters: "Alas! I am the cause of all this trouble."

The nuns, turning in amazement, saw that it was Kwan-yin who was speaking. "You?" they exclaimed, astounded.

"Yes, I, for I am indeed the daughter of a king. My father did not wish me to take the vows of this holy order. I fled from the palace. He has sent his army here to burn these buildings and to drag me back a prisoner."

"Then, see what you have brought upon us, miserable girl!" exclaimed the abbess. "See how you have repaid our kindness! Our buildings will be burned above our heads! How wretched you have made us! May heaven's curses rest upon you!"

"No, no!" exclaimed Kwan-yin, springing up, and trying to keep the abbess from speaking these frightful words. "You have no right to say that, for I am innocent of evil. But, wait! You shall soon see whose prayers the gods will answer, yours or mine!"

So saying, she pressed her forehead to the floor, praying the almighty powers to save the convent and the sisters.

Outside the crackling of the greedy flames could already be heard. The fire king would soon destroy every building on that hilltop. Mad with terror, the sisters prepared to leave the compound and give up all their belongings to the cruel flames and still more cruel soldiers. Kwan-yin alone remained in the room, praying earnestly for help.

Suddenly a soft breeze sprang up from the neighboring forest, dark clouds gathered overhead, and, although it was the dry season a drenching shower descended on the flames. Within five minutes the fire was put out and the convent was saved. Just as the shivering nuns were thanking Kwan-yin for the divine help she had brought them, two soldiers who had scaled the outer wall of the compound came in and roughly asked for the princess.

The trembling girl, knowing that these men were obeying her father's orders, poured out a prayer to the gods, and straightway made herself known. They dragged her from the presence of the nuns who had just begun to love her. Thus disgraced before her father's army, she was taken to the capital.

On the morrow, she was led before the old king. The father gazed sadly at his daughter, and then the stern look of a judge hardened his face as he beckoned the guards to bring her forward.

From a neighboring room came the sounds of sweet music. A feast was being served there amid great splendor. The loud laughter of the guests reached the ears of the young girl as she bowed in disgrace before her father's throne. She knew that this feast had been prepared for her, and that her father was willing to give her one more chance.

"Girl," said the king, at last regaining his voice, "in leaving the royal palace on the eve of your wedding day, not only did you insult your father, but your king. For this act you deserve to die. However, because of the excellent record you had made for yourself before you ran away, I have decided to give you one more chance to redeem yourself. Refuse me, and the penalty is death: obey me, and all may yet be well the kingdom that you spurned is still yours for the asking. All that I require is your marriage to the man whom I have chosen."

"And when, most august King, would you have me decide?" asked Kwan-yin earnestly.

"This very day, this very hour, this very moment," he answered sternly. "What! would you hesitate between love upon a throne and death? Speak, my daughter, tell me that you love me and will do my bidding!"

It was now all that Kwan-yin could do to keep from throwing herself at her father's feet and yielding to his wishes, not because he offered her a kingdom, but because she loved him and would gladly have made him happy. But her strong will kept her from relenting. No power on earth could have stayed her from doing what she thought her duty.

"Beloved father," she answered sadly, and her voice was full of tenderness, "it is not a question of my love for you of that there is no question, for all my life I have shown it in every action. Believe me, if I were free to do your bidding, gladly would I make you happy, but a voice from the gods has spoken, has commanded that I remain a virgin, that I devote my life to deeds of mercy. When heaven itself has commanded, what can even a princess do but listen to that power which rules the earth?"

The old king was far from satisfied with Kwan-yin's answer. He grew furious, his thin wrinkled skin turned purple as the hot blood rose to his head. "Then you refuse to do my bidding! Take her, men! Give to her the death that is due to a traitor to the king!" As they bore Kwan-yin away from his presence the white-haired monarch fell, swooning, from his chair.

That night, when Kwan-yin was put to death, she descended into the lower world of torture. No sooner had she set foot in that dark country of the dead than the vast region of endless punishment suddenly blossomed forth and became like the gardens of Paradise. Pure white lilies sprang up on every side, and the odour of a million flowers filled all the rooms and corridors. King Yama, ruler of the dominion, rushed forth to learn the cause of this wonderful change. No sooner did his eyes rest upon the fair young face of Kwan-yin than he saw in her the emblem of a purity which deserved no home but heaven.

"Beautiful virgin, doer of many mercies," he began, after addressing her by her title, "I beg you in the name of justice to depart from this bloody kingdom. It is not right that the fairest flower of heaven should enter and shed her fragrance in these halls. Guilt must suffer here, and sin find no reward. Depart thou, then, from my dominion. The peach of immortal life shall be bestowed upon you, and heaven alone shall be your dwelling place."

Thus Kwan-yin became the Goddess of Mercy; thus she entered into that glad abode, surpassing all earthly kings and queens. And ever since that time, on account of her exceeding goodness, thousands of poor people breathe out to her each year their prayers for mercy. There is no fear in their gaze as they look at her beautiful image, for their eyes are filled with tears of love.

Source: "The Princess Kwan-Yin," Norman Hinsdale Pitman. *A Chinese Wonder Book.* (New York: E.P. Dutton, 1919), pp. 133–146.

The Great Gambling Match

The following tale is an episode from the great Hindu epic, The Mahabharata (The Story of the Bharata). *The epic describes the bitter rivalry
between two sets of cousins, the Pandavas and the Kauravas, a rivalry
that ultimately erupts into a war over the kingdom of Bharata. The
Mahabharata is a source of ethical, genealogical, and theological
wisdom that forms the core of Hindu religion worldwide. In the following excerpt, Duryodhana (of the Kauravas), the major antagonist of the
work, launches a conspiracy to humiliate his Pandava rivals.*

Now Shakuni, Prince of Gandhara, and brother of Dhritarashtra's queen,
was renowned for his skill as a gambler. He always enjoyed good fortune
because that he played with loaded dice. Duryodhana plotted with him,
desiring greatly to subjugate the Pandavas, and Shakuni said: "Be advised
by me. Yudhishthira loves the dice, although he knows not how to play.
Ask him to throw dice with me, for there is no gambler who is my equal in
the three worlds. I will put him to shame. I will win from him his kingdom,
O bull among men."

Duryodhana was well pleased at this proposal, and he went before his
blind father, the maharajah, and prevailed upon him to invite the Pandavas
to Hastinapur for a friendly gambling match, despite the warnings of the
royal counselors.

Said Dhritarashtra: "If the gods are merciful, my sons will cause no
dispute. Let it be as fate hath ordained. No evil can happen so long as I am
near, and Bhishma and Drona are near also. Therefore, let the Pandavas be
invited hither as my son desireth."

So Vidura, who feared trouble, was sent unto Indra-prastha to say:
"The maharajah is about to hold a great festival at Hastinapur, and he
desires that Yudhishthira and his brethren, their mother Pritha and their
joint wife Draupadi, should be present. A great gambling match will be
played."

When Yudhishthira heard these words, he sorrowed greatly, for well he
knew that dice-throwing was ofttimes the cause of bitter strife. Besides, he
was unwilling to play Prince Shakuni, that desperate and terrible gambler....
But he could not refuse the invitation of Dhritarashtra, or, like a true

Kshatriya [warrior-aristocrat], disdain a challenge either to fight or to play with his peers.

So it came to pass that the Pandava brethren, with Pritha, their mother, and their joint wife Draupadi, journeyed to Hastinapur in all their splendour. Dhritarashtra welcomed them in the presence of Bhishma and Drona and Duryodhana and Karna; then they were received by Queen Gandhari, and the wives of the Kaurava princes; and all the daughters-in-law of the blind maharajah became sad because that they were jealous of the beauty of Draupadi and the splendour of her attire.

The Pandava lords and ladies went unto the dwelling which had been prepared for them, and there they were visited in turn by the lords and ladies of Hastinapur.

On the day that followed, Yudhishthira and his brethren went together to the gambling match, which was held in a gorgeous pavilion, roofed with arching crystal and decorated with gold and lapis lazuli: it had a hundred doors and a thousand great columns, and it was richly carpeted. All the princes and great chieftains and warriors of the kingdom were gathered there. And Prince Shakuni of Gandhari was there also with his false dice.

When salutations had passed, and the great company were seated, Shakuni invited Yudhishthira to play.

Said Yudhishthira: "I will play if mine opponent will promise to throw fairly, without trickery and deceit. Deceitful gambling is sinful, and unworthy a Kshatriya; there is no prowess in it. Wise men do not applaud a player who winneth by foul means."

Shakuni said: "A skilled gambler ever playeth with purpose to vanquish his opponent, as one warrior fighteth another less skilled than himself to accomplish his over-throw. Such is the practice in all contests; a man plays or fights to achieve victory....But if thou art in dread of me, O Yudhishthira, and afraid that thou wilt lose, 'twere better if thou didst not play at all."

Said Yudhishthira: "Having been challenged, I cannot withdraw. I fear not to fight or to play with any man....But first say who doth challenge and who is to lay stakes equally with me."

Then Duryodhana spoke, saying: "O rajah, I will supply jewels and gold and any stakes thou wilt of as great value as thou canst set down. It is for me that Shakuni, my uncle, is to throw the dice."

Said Yudhishthira: "This is indeed a strange challenge. One man is to throw the dice and another is to lay the stakes. Such is contrary to all practice. If, however, thou art determined to play in this fashion, let the game begin."

Well did the Rajah of Indra-prastha know then that the match would not be played fairly. But he sat down, notwithstanding, to throw dice with Shakuni.

At the first throw Yudhishthira lost; indeed, he lost at every throw on that fatal day. He gambled away all his money and all his jewels, his jeweled chariot with golden bells, and all his cattle; still he played on, and he lost his thousand war elephants, his slaves and beautiful slave girls, and the remainder of his goods; and next, he staked and lost the whole kingdom of the Pandavas, save the lands which he had gifted to the Brahmans. Nor did he cease to play then, despite the advice offered him by the chieftains who were there. One by one he staked and lost his brethren; and he staked himself and lost also.

Said Shakuni: "You have done ill, Yudhishthira, in staking thine own self; for now thou hast become a slave; but if thou wilt stake Draupadi now and win, all that thou hast lost will be restored unto thee."

Yudhishthira said: "So be it. I will stake Draupadi."

At these words the whole company was stricken with horror. Vidura swooned, and the faces of Bhishma and Drona grew pallid; many groaned; but Duryodhana and his brethren rejoiced openly before all men.

Shakuni threw the dice, and Yudhishthira lost this the last throw. In this manner was Draupadi won by Duryodhana.

Then all the onlookers gazed one upon another in silence and wide-eyed. Karna and Duhsasana and other young princes laughed aloud.

Duryodhana rose proudly and spake unto Vidura, saying: "Now hasten unto Draupadi and bid her to come hither to sweep the chambers with the other bonds-women."

Vidura was made angry, and answered him: "Thy words are wicked, O Duryodhana. Thou canst not command a lady of royal birth to become a household slave. Besides, she is not thy slave, because Yudhishthira would stake his own freedom before he staked Draupadi. Thou couldst not win aught from a slave who had no power to stake the princess."

But Duryodhana cursed Vidura, and bade one of his servants to bring Draupadi before him.

Said Vidura: "Duryodhana is this day deprived of his reason. Dishonesty is one of the doors to hell. By practicing dishonesty Duryodhana will accomplish yet the ruin of the Kauravas."

The beautiful Draupadi was sitting at peace within the fair dwelling set apart for the Pandavas on the banks of the Ganges; its walls and towers were mirrored on the broad clear waters. Then suddenly, as a jackal enters stealthily the den of a lion, the menial sent by Duryodhana entered the palace and stood before high-born Draupadi.

Said this man: "O queen, the mighty son of Pandu hath played and lost; he hath lost all, even his reason, and he hath staked thee, and thou hast been won by Duryodhana. And now Duryodhana bids me to say that thou art become his slave, and must obey him like to other female slaves. So come thou with me, for thou must henceforth engage in menial work."

Draupadi was astounded when he spake these words, and in her anguish she cried: "Have I heard thee aright? Hath my husband, the king, staked and lost me in his madness? Did he stake and loose aught beside?"

Said the man: "Yudhishthira hath lost all his riches and his kingdom; he staked his brethren and lost them one by one; he staked himself and lost; and then he staked thee, O queen, and lost also. Therefore, come thou with me."

Draupadi rose in her pride and spoke angrily, saying: "If my lord did stake himself and become a slave, he could not wager me, for a slave owns neither his own life nor the life of another. Speak, therefore, unto my husband these words, and unto Duryodhana say: 'Draupadi hath not been won'."

The man returned to the assembly and spake unto Yudhishthira the words which Draupadi had said, but he bowed his head and was silent.

Duryodhana was made angry by the defiant answer of the proud queen, and he said unto his brother Duhsasana: "The sons of Pandu are our slaves, and thy heart is without fear for them. Go thou to the palace and bid the princess, my humble menial, to come hither quickly."

Red-eyed and proud Duhsasana hastened to the palace. He entered the inner chambers and stood before Draupadi, who was clad in but a single robe, while her hair hung loosely.

Said the evil-hearted Kaurava: "O princess of Panchala with fair lotus eyes, thou hast been staked and lost fairly at the game of hazard. Hasten, therefore, and stand before thy lord Duryodhana, for thou art now his bright-eyed slave."

Draupadi heard and trembled. She covered her eyes with her hands before the hated Duhsasana; her cheeks turned pale and her heart sickened. Then suddenly she leapt up and sought to escape to an inner room. But the evil-hearted prince seized her by the hair, for he no longer feared the sons of Pandu, and the beautiful princess quivered and shook in her loose attire like to a sapling which is shaken by the storm wind. Crouching on her knees, she cried angrily, while tears streamed from her lotus eyes: "Begone! O shameless prince. Can a modest woman appear before strangers in loose attire?"

Said stern and cruel Duhsasana: "Even if thou wert naked now, thou must follow me. Hast thou not become a slave, fairly staked and fairly won? Henceforth thou wilt serve among the other menials."

Trembling and faint, Draupadi was dragged through the streets by Duhsasana. When she stood before the elders and the chieftains in the pavilion she cried: "Forgive me because that I have come hither in this unseemly plight...."

Bhishma and Drona and the other elders who were there hung their heads in shame.

Unto Duhsasana Draupadi said angrily: "Cease thy wickedness! Defile me no longer with unclean hands. A woman's hair is sacred."

Sacred indeed were the locks of the Pandava queen, for they had been sprinkled with water sanctified by mantras at the imperial sacrifice.

Weeping, she cried: "Hear and help me, O ye elders. You have wives and children of your own. Will you permit this wrong to be continued. Answer me now."

But no man spake a word.

Draupadi wept and said: "Why this silence?...Will no man among ye protect a sinless woman?...Lost is the fame of the Kauravas, the ancient glory of Bharata, and the prowess of the Kshatriyas!...Why will not the sons of Pandu protect their outraged queen?...And hath Bhishma lost his virtue and Drona his power?...Will Yudhishthira no longer defend one who is wronged?...Why are ye all silent while this deed of shame is done before you?"

As she spake thus, Draupadi glanced round the sons of Pandu one by one, and their hearts thirsted for vengeance. Bhishma's face was dark, Drona clenched his teeth, and Vidura, white and angry, gazed upon Duhsasana with amaze while he tore off Draupadi's veil and addressed her with foul words. When she looked towards the Kaurava brethren, Duhsasana said: "Ha! on whom darest thou to look now, O slave?"

Shakuni and Karna laughed to hear Draupadi called a slave, and they cried out: "Well spoken, well spoken!"

Duhsasana endeavoured to strip the princess naked before the assembly; but Draupadi, in her distress, prayed aloud to Krishna, invoking him as the creator of all and the soul of the universe, and entreated him to help her. Krishna heard her, and multiplied her garments so that Duhsasana was unable to accomplish his wicked purpose.

Karna spake to Draupadi and said: "'Tis not thy blame, O princess, that thou hast fallen so low. A woman's fate is controlled by her husband; Yudhishthira hath gambled thee away. Thou wert his, and must accept thy fate. Henceforward thou wilt be the slave of the Kaurava princes. Thou must obey them and please them with thy beauty.'Tis meet that thou shouldst now seek for thyself a husband who will love thee too well to stake thee at dice and suffer thee to be put to shame....Be assured that no one will blame a humble menial, as thou now art, who looks with eyes of love upon great and noble warriors. Remember that Yudhishthira is no longer thy husband; he hath become a slave, and a slave can have no wife....Ah! sweet Princess of Panchala, those whom thou didst choose have gambled and lost thee; their kingdom they have lost, and their power also."

At these words Bhima's bosom heaved with anger and with shame. Red-eyed he scowled upon Karna; he seemed to be the image of flaming Wrath. Unto Yudhishthira he spake grimly, saying: "If you hadst not staked our freedom and our queen, O king and elder brother, this son of a chari-oteer would not have taunted us in this manner."

Yudhishthira bowed his head in shame, nor answered a word. Arjuna reproved Bhima for his bitter words; but Pritha's mighty son, the slayer of Asuras, said: "If I am not permitted to punish the tormentor of Draupadi, bring me a fire that I may thrust my hands into it."

A deep uproar rose from the assembly, and the elders applauded the wronged lady and censured Duhsasana. Bhima clenched his hands and, with quivering lips, cried out: "Hear my terrible words, O ye Kshatriyas....May I never reach Heaven if I do not yet seize Duhsasana in battle and, tearing open his breast, drink his very life blood!..."

Again he spoke and said: "If Yudhishthira will permit me, I will slay the wretched sons of Dhritarashtra without weapons, even as a lion slays small animals."

Then Bhishma and Vidura and Drona cried out: "Forbear, O Bhima! Everything is possible in thee."

Duryodhana gloried in his hour of triumph, and unto the elder of the Pandava brethren spake tauntingly and said: "Yudhishthira, thou art spokesman for thy brethren, and they owe thee obedience. Speak and say, thou who dost ever speak truly, hast thou lost thy kingdom and thy brethren and thine own self? O Yudhishthira, hast thou lost even the beauteous Draupadi? And hath she, thy wedded wife, become our humble menial?"

Yudhishthira heard him with downcast eyes, but his lips moved not.... Then Karna laughed; but Bhishma, pious and old, wept in silence.

Then Duryodhana cast burning eyes upon Draupadi, and, baring his knee, invited her, as a slave, to sit upon it.

Bhima gnashed his teeth, for he was unable to restrain his pent-up anger. With eyes flashing like lightning, and in a voice like to thunder he cried out: "Hear my vow! May I never reach Heaven or meet my ancestors hereafter if, for these deeds of sin, I do not break the knee of Duryodhana in battle, and drink the blood of Duhsasana!"

The flames of wrath which leapt on the forehead of Bhima were like red sparks flying from tough branches on a crackling fire.

Dhritarashtra was sitting in his palace, nor knew aught of what was passing. The Brahmans, robed in white, were chanting peacefully their evening mantras, when a jackal howled in the sacrificial chamber. Asses brayed in response, and ravens answered their cries from all sides. Those who heard these dread omens exclaimed: "*Swashti! Swashti!* [Amen! Amen!]."

Dhritarashtra shook with terror, and when Vidura had told him all that had taken place, he said: "The luckless and sinful Duryodhana hath brought shame upon the head of Rajah Drupada's sweet daughter, and thus courted death and destruction. May the prayers of a sorrowful old man remove the wrath of Heaven which these dark omens have revealed."

Then the blind maharajah was led to Draupadi, and before all the elders and the princes he spoke to her, kindly and gently, and said: "Noble queen and virtuous daughter, wife of pious Yudhishthira, and purest of all women, thou art very dear unto my heart. Alas! My sons have wronged thee in foul manner this day. O forgive them now, and let the wrath of Heaven be averted. Whatsoever thou wilt ask of me will be thine."

Said Draupadi: "O mighty maharajah, thou art merciful; may happiness be thy dower. I ask of thee to set at liberty now my lord and husband Yudhishthira. Having been a prince, it is not seemly that he should be called a slave."

Dhritarashtra said: "Thy wish is granted. Ask a second boon and blessing, O fair one. Thou dost deserve more than a single boon."

Said Draupadi: "Let Arjuna and Bhima and their younger brethren be set free also and allowed to depart now with their horses and their chariots and their weapons."

Dhritarashtra said: "So be it, O high-born princess. Ask yet another boon and blessing and it will be granted thee."

Said Draupadi: "I seek no other boon, thou generous monarch: I am a Kshatriya by birth, and not like to a Brahman, who craveth for gifts without end. Thou hast freed my husbands from slavery: they will regain their fortunes by their own mighty deeds."

Then the Pandava brethren departed from Hastinapur with Pritha and Draupadi, and returned unto the city of Indra-prastha.

The Kauravas were made angry, and Duryodhana remonstrated with his royal sire and said: "Thou hast permitted the Pandava princes to depart in their anger; now they will make ready to wage war against us to regain their kingdom and their wealth; when they return they will slay us all. Permit us, therefore, to throw dice with them once again. We will stake our liberty, and be it laid down that the side which loseth shall go into exile for twelve full years, and into concealment for a year thereafter. By this arrangement a bloody war may be averted."

Dhritarashtra granted his son's wish and recalled the Pandavas. So it came to pass that Yudhishthira sat down once again to play with Shakuni, and once again Shakuni brought forth the loaded dice. Ere long the game ended, and Yudhishthira had lost.

Duhsasana danced with joy and cried aloud: "Now is established the empire of Duryodhana."

Said Bhima: "Be not too gladsome, O Duhsasana. Hear and remember my words: May I never reach Heaven or meet my sires until I shall drink thy blood!"

Then the Pandava princes cast off their royal garments and clad themselves in deerskins like humble mendicants. Yudhishthira bade farewell to Dhritarashtra and Bhishma and Kripa and Vidura, one by one, and he even said farewell to the Kaurava brethren.

Said Vidura: "Thy mother, the royal Pritha, is too old to wander with thee through forest and jungle. Let her dwell here until the years of your exile have passed away.

Yudhishthira spoke for his brethren and said: "Be it so, O saintly Vidura. Now bless us ere we depart, for thou hast been unto us like to a father."

Then Vidura blessed each one of the Pandava princes, saying: "Be saintly in exile, subdue your passions, learn truth in your sorrow, and return in happiness. May these eyes be blessed by beholding thee in Hastinapur once again."

Pritha wept over Draupadi and blessed her. Then the Princess of Panchala went forth with loose tresses; but ere she departed from the city she vowed a vow, saying: "From this day my hair will fall over my forehead until Bhima shall have slain Duhsasana and drunk his blood; then shall Bhima tie up my tresses while his hands are yet wet with the blood of Duhsasana."

The Pandava princes wandered towards the deep forest, and Draupadi followed them.

Source: "The Great Gambling Match," Donald A. Mackenzie. *Indian Myth and Legend.* (London: The Gresham Publishing Company Limited, 1913), pp. 237–248.

The Monkey and the Turtle

Filipino Americans report that, while some of the tales from this Southeast Asian tradition have faded in the contemporary United States, the fable of "The Monkey and the Turtle" has been preserved. The narrative of the origin of enmity between turtles and monkeys casts Monkey in the role of deceitful exploiter. Monkey's treachery is punished by Turtle who then uses the classic trickster's ploy of begging for any judgment except the one he really wishes Monkey to decree.

One day, a Monkey met a Turtle on the road, and asked, "Where are you going?"

"I am going to find something to eat, for I have had no food for three whole days," said the Turtle.

"I too am hungry," said the Monkey; "and since we are both hungry, let us go together and hunt food for our stomachs' sake."

They soon became good friends and chatted along the way, so that the time passed quickly. Before they had gone far, the Monkey saw a large bunch of yellow bananas on a tree at a distance.

"Oh, what a good sight that is!" cried he. "Don't you see the bananas hanging on that banana-tree? They are fine! I can taste them already."

But the Turtle was short-sighted and could not see them. By and by they came near the tree, and then he saw them. The two friends were very glad. The mere sight of the ripe, yellow fruit seemed to assuage their hunger.

But the Turtle could not climb the tree, so he agreed that the Monkey should go up alone and should throw some of the fruit down to him. The Monkey was up in a flash; and, seating himself comfortably, he began to eat the finest of the fruit, and forgot to drop any down to the Turtle waiting below. The Turtle called for some, but the Monkey pretended not to hear. He ate even the peelings, and refused to drop a bit to his friend, who was patiently begging under the tree.

At last the Turtle became angry, very angry indeed: so he thought he would get revenge. While the Monkey was having a good time, and filling his stomach, the Turtle gathered sharp, broken pieces of glass, and stuck them, one by one, all around the banana-tree. Then he hid himself under a cocoanut-shell not far away. This shell had a hole in the top to allow the air to enter. That was why the Turtle chose it for his hiding-place.

The Monkey could not eat all the bananas, for there were enough to last a good-sized family several days; but he ate all that he can, and by and by came down the tree with great difficulty, for the glass was so sharp that it cut even the tough hand of the Monkey. He had a hard time, and his hands were cut in many places. The Turtle thought he had his revenge, and was not so angry as before.

But the Monkey was now very angry at the trick that had been played upon him, and began looking for the Turtle, intending to kill him. For some time he could not find his foe, and, being very tired, he sat down on the coconut shell near by. His weariness increased his anger at the Turtle very much.

He sat on the shell for a long time, suffering from his wounds, and wondering where to find the Turtle, his former friend, but now his enemy. Because of the disturbance of the shell, the Turtle inside could not help making a noise. This the Monkey heard, and he was surprised, for he could not determine whence the sound came. At last he lifted his stool, and there found his foe the Turtle.

"Ha! Here you are!" he cried. "Pray now, for it is the end of your life."

He picked up the Turtle by the neck and carried him near the river-bank, where he meant to kill him. He took a mortar and pestle, and built a big fire, intending to pound him to powder or burn him to death. When everything was ready, he told the Turtle to choose whether he should die in the fire or be ground in the mortar. The Turtle begged for his life; but when he found it was in vain, he prayed to be thrown into the fire or ground in the mortar, anything except be thrown into the water. On hearing this, the Monkey picked the Turtle up in his bleeding fingers, and with all his might threw him into the middle of the stream.

Then the Turtle was very glad. He chuckled at his own wit, and laughed at the foolishness of the Monkey. He came up to the surface of the water and mocked at the Monkey, saying, "This is my home. The water is my home."

This made the Monkey so angry that he lost his self-possession entirely. He jumped into the middle of the river after the Turtle, and was drowned.

Since that day monkeys and turtles have been bitter enemies.

Source: "The Monkey and the Turtle," Clara Kern Bayliss, "Philippine Folk-Tales." *Journal of American Folklore* 21 (1908): pp. 46–53, 46–47.

Why Dogs Wag Their Tails

Animal tales, conscious fictions using animal characters exhibiting human traits, comprise an important segment of Filipino traditional folklore. Some conclude with a moral lesson in the form of a proverb. Others, like the following example, offer a humorous explanation for a common phenomenon.

Once upon a time there lived in a certain village a rich man who had a dog and a cat. His only daughter, of whom he was very fond, was studying in a convent in a city several miles distant, and it was his custom, about once a week, to send the dog and cat to take her a little present. The dog was so old that he had lost all his teeth, and so was unable to fight, but the cat was strong and very cunning, and so one could help the other, since the dog knew better how to find the way.

One day the rich man wished to send a magic ring to his daughter, so he called the dog and the cat to him. To the cat he said, "You are very cunning and prudent. You may carry this magic ring to my daughter, but be sure to take very great care of it." To the dog he said, "You are to go with the cat to take a magic ring to my daughter. Take care not to lose the way, and see that no one molests the cat." Both animals promised to do their best and set out immediately.

On the way they were obliged to cross a wide and deep river, over which there was no bridge, and as they were unable to find a boat, they determined to swim across it.

The dog said to the cat, "Give me the magic ring."

"Oh, no," replied the cat. "Did you not hear the master say just what each of us had to do?"

"Yes, but you are not very good at swimming, and may lose the ring, while I am strong and can take good care of it," answered the dog. The cat continued to refuse to disobey its master, until at last the dog threatened to kill it, and it was obliged to entrust the ring to the dog's keeping.

Then they began to swim across the river, which was so strong that they were about an hour in getting over, so that both became very tired and weak. Just before they came to the other side, the dog dropped the ring into the water, and it was impossible to find it.

"Now," said the cat, "we had better go back home and tell our master that we have lost the ring."

"Yes," answered the dog, "but I am very much afraid." So they turned back toward home, but as they drew near the house his fear so overcame him that he ran away and was never seen again.

The master was very much surprised to see the cat back so soon, and asked him, "Where is your companion?"

The cat was at first afraid to answer. "Where is the dog?" asked the master again.

"Oh, he ran away," replied the cat.

"Ran away?" said the master. "What do you mean? Where is the ring?"

"Oh, pardon me, my master," answered the cat. "Do not be angry, and I will tell you what has happened. When we reached the bank of the river, the dog asked me to give him the ring. This I refused many times, until at last he threatened to kill me if I did not give it to him, and I was obliged to do so. The river was very hard to cross, and on the way the dog dropped the ring into the water and we could not find it. I persuaded the dog to come back with me to tell you about it, but on the way he became so frightened that he ran away."

Then the master made a proclamation to the people, offering a reward to the one who should find his old dog and bring him to him. They could recognize the dog by his being old and having no teeth. The master also declared that when he had found the delinquent he would punish him by cutting off his tail. He ordered that the dogs all around the world should take part in the search, and so ever since that time, when one dog meets another he always asks: "Are you the old dog who lost the magic ring? If you are, your tail must be cut off." Then instantly both show their teeth and wag their tails to mean no. Since that time, also, cats have been afraid of water, and will never swim across a river if it can be avoided.

Source: "Why Dogs Wag Their Tails," Berton L. Maxfield and W.H. Millington, "Visayan Folk-Tales II." *Journal of American Folklore* 20 (1907): pp. 89–103, 98–100.

The Casting of the Great Bell

Among adherents to the Confucian philosophical system as practiced in China and in the Chinese American community, filial piety (respect of a child for his or her parents) is among the greatest virtues. Narratives such as the following legend serve as models of this devotion, although contemporary Chinese Americans would not advocate the extremes to which this dedication is said to have been carried in historical contexts.

In every province of China there is a legend relating to the casting of the great bell swung in the bell tower of the chief city. These legends are curiously identical in almost every detail. The following is the one current in Peking.

It was in the reign of Yung Lo, the third monarch of the Ming dynasty, that Peking first became the capital of China. Till that period the 'Son of Heaven' had held his Court at Nanking, and Peking had been of comparatively little note. Now, however, on being honoured by the 'Sacred Presence,' stately buildings arose in all directions for the accommodation of the Emperor and his courtiers. Clever men from all parts of the Empire were attracted to the capital, and such as possessed talent were sure of lucrative employment. About this time the Drum Tower and the Bell Tower were built; both of them as 'look-out' and 'alarm' towers. The Drum Tower was furnished with a monster drum, which it still possesses, of such a size that the thunder of its tones might be heard all over the city, the sound being almost enough to waken the dead. The Bell Tower had been completed some time before attempts were made to cast a bell proportionate to the size of the building.

At length Yung Lo ordered Kuan Yu, a mandarin of the second grade, who was skilled in casting guns, to cast a bell the sound of which should be heard, on the least alarm, in every part of the city. Kuan Yu at once commenced the undertaking. He secured the services of a great number of experienced workmen, and collected immense quantities of material. Months passed, and at length it was announced to the Emperor that everything was ready for the casting. A day was appointed; the Emperor, surrounded by a crowd of courtiers, and preceded by the Court musicians, went to witness the ceremony. At a given signal, and to the crash of music, the melted metal rushed into the mould prepared for it. The Emperor and his Court then retired, leaving Kuan Yu and his subordinates to await the cooling of the metal, which would tell of failure or success. At length the metal was sufficiently cool to detach the mould from it. Kuan Yu, in breathless trepidation, hastened to inspect it, but to his mortification and grief discovered it to be honeycombed in many places. The circumstance was reported to the Emperor, who was naturally vexed at the expenditure of so much time, labour, and money with so unsatisfactory a result. However, he ordered Kuan Yu to try again.

The mandarin hastened to obey, and, thinking the failure of the first attempt must have resulted from some oversight or omission on his part, he watched every detail with redoubled care and attention, fully determined that no neglect or remissness should mar the success of this second casting.

After months of labour the mould was again prepared, and the metal poured into it, but again with the same result. Kuan Yu was distracted, not only at the loss of his reputation, but at the certain loss of the Emperor's favour. Yung Lo, when he heard of this second failure, was very wroth, and at once ordered Kuan Yu into his presence, and told him he would give him a third and last trial, and if he did not succeed this time he would behead him. Kuan Yu went home in a despairing state of mind, asking himself what crime he or any of his ancestors could have committed to have justified this calamity.

Now Kuan Yu had an only daughter, about sixteen years of age, and, having no sons, the whole of his love was centred in this girl, for he had hopes of perpetuating his name and fame through her marriage with some deserving young nobleman. Truly she was worthy of being loved. She had "almond-shaped eyes, like the autumn waves, which, sparkling and dancing in the sun, seem to leap up in very joy and wantonness to kiss the fragrant reeds that grow upon the rivers' banks, yet of such limpid transparency that one's form could be seen in their liquid depths as if reflected in a mirror. These were surrounded by long silken lashes—now drooping in coy modesty, anon rising in youthful gaiety and disclosing the laughing eyes but just before concealed beneath them. Eyebrows like the willow leaf; cheeks of snowy whiteness, yet tinged with the gentlest colouring of the rose; teeth like pearls of the finest water were seen peeping from between half-open lips, so luscious and juicy that they resembled two cherries; hair of the jettiest blackness and of the silkiest texture. Her form was such as poets love to describe and painters limn; there was grace and ease in every movement; she appeared to glide rather than walk, so light was she of foot. Add to her other charms that she was skilful in verse-making, excellent in embroidery, and unequalled in the execution of her household duties, and we have but a faint description of Ko-ai, the beautiful daughter of Kuan Yu."

Well might the father be proud of and love his beautiful child, and she returned his love with all the ardour of her affectionate nature; often cheering him with her innocent gaiety when he returned from his daily vocations wearied or vexed. Seeing him now return with despair depicted in his countenance, she tenderly inquired the cause, not without hope of being the means of alleviating it. When her father told her of his failures, and of the Emperor's threat, she exclaimed: "Oh, my father, be comforted! Heaven will not always be thus unrelenting. Are we not told that 'out of evil cometh good'? These two failures will but enhance the glory of your eventual success, for success *this* time *must* crown your efforts. I am only a girl, and cannot assist you but with my prayers; these I will daily and hourly offer up for your success; and the prayers of a daughter for a loved parent *must* be heard."

Somewhat soothed by the endearments of Ko-ai, Kuan Yu again devoted himself to his task with redoubled energy, Ko-ai meanwhile constantly praying for him in his absence, and ministering to his wants when he returned home.

One day it occurred to the maiden to go to a celebrated astrologer to ascertain the cause of these failures, and to ask what means could be taken to prevent a recurrence of them. She thus learned that the next casting would also be a disappointment if the blood of a maiden were not mixed with the ingredients. She returned home full of horror at this information, yet inwardly resolving to immolate herself rather than allow her father to fail. The day for the casting at length came, and Ko-ai requested her father to allow her to witness the ceremony and "to exult in his success," as she laughingly said. Kuan Yu gave his consent, and accompanied by several servants she went, taking up a position near the mould.

Everything was prepared as before. An immense concourse assembled to witness the third and final casting, which was to result either in honor or degradation and death for Kuan Yu. A dead silence prevailed through the vast assemblage as the melted metal once more rushed to its destination; this was broken by a shriek, and a cry, "For my father!" and Ko-ai was seen to throw herself headlong into the seething, hissing metal. One of her servants attempted to seize her while in the act of plunging into the boiling fluid, but succeeded only in grasping one of her shoes, which came off in his hand. The father was frantic, and had to be kept by force from following her example; he was taken home a raving maniac. The prediction of the astrologer was fulfilled, for, on uncovering the bell after it had cooled, it was found to be perfect, but not a vestige of Ko-ai was to be seen; the blood of a maiden had indeed been infused with the ingredients.

After a time the bell was suspended by order of the Emperor, and expectation was at its height to hear it rung for the first time. The Emperor himself was present. The bell was struck, and far and near was heard the deep tone of its sonorous boom. This indeed was a triumph! Here was a bell surpassing in size and sound any other that had ever been cast! But—and the surrounding multitudes were horror-struck as they listened—the heavy boom of the bell was followed by a low wailing sound like the agonized cry of a woman, and the word *hsieh* (shoe) was distinctly heard. To this day the bell, each time it is rung, after every boom appears to utter the word 'hsieh,' and people when they hear it shudder and say, "There's poor Ko-ai's voice calling for her shoe."

Source: "The Casting of the Great Bell," Edward T.C. Werner. *Myths and Legends of China*. (London: George G. Harrap & Co., 1922), pp. 392–398.

The Geomancer

Although in the contemporary United States geomancy (divination by means of the earth) through the popularity of feng shui (literally "wind-water") is generally associated with traditional Chinese culture or New Age philosophy, this form of divination has been practiced in Korea since the Three Kingdoms Period (57 B.C.E.–668 C.E.). Both the art and the art's folk history are elements of the Korean American heritage.

Yi Eui-sin was a specialist in Geomancy. His craft came into being evidently as a by-product of Taoism, but has had mixed in it elements of ancient Chinese philosophy. The Positive and the Negative, the Two Primary Principles in Nature, play a great part; also the Five Elements, Metal, Wood, Water, Fire and Earth. In the selection of a site, that for a house is called a "male" choice, while the grave is denominated the "female" choice.

Millions of money have been expended in Korea on the geomancer and his associates in the hope of finding lucky homes for the living and auspicious resting-places for the dead, the Korean idea being that, in some mysterious way, all our fortune is associated with Mother Earth.

The Story

There was a geomancer once, Yi Eui-sin, who in seeking out a special mountain vein, started with the Dragon Ridge in North Ham-kyong Province, and traced it as far as Pine Mountain in Yang-ju County, where it stopped in a beautifully rounded end, forming a perfect site for burial. After wandering all day in the hills, Yi's hungry spirit cried out for food.

He saw beneath the hill a small house, to which he went, and rapping at the door asked for something to eat. A mourner, recently bereaved, came out in a respectful and kindly way, and gave him a dish of white gruel.

Yi, after he had eaten, asked what time the friend had become a mourner, and if he had already passed the funeral. The owner answered, "I am just now entering upon full mourning, but we have not yet arranged for the funeral." He spoke in a sad and disheartened way.

Yi felt sorry for him, and asked the reason. "I wonder if it's because you are poor that you have not yet made the necessary arrangements, or perhaps you have not yet found a suitable site! I am an expert in reading the hills, and I'll tell you of a site; would you care to see it?"

The mourner thanked him most gratefully, and said, "I'll be delighted to know of it." Yi then showed him the end of the great vein that he had just discovered, also the spot for the grave and how to place its compass points. "After possessing this site," said he, "you will be greatly enriched, but in ten years you will have cause to arrange for another site. When that comes to pass please call me, won't you? In calling for me just ask for Yi So-pang, who lives in West School Ward, Seoul."

The mourner did as directed, and as the geomancer had foretold, all his affairs prospered. He built a large tiled house, and ornamented the grave with great stones as a prosperous and high-minded country gentleman should do.

After ten years a guest called one day, and saluting him asked, "Is that grave yonder, beyond the stream, yours?"

The master answered, "It is mine."

Then the stranger said, "That is a famous site, but ten years have passed since you have come into possession of it, and the luck is gone; why do you not make a change ? If you wait too long you will rue it and may meet with great disaster."

The owner, hearing this, thought of Yi the geomancer, and what he had said years before. Remembering that, he asked the stranger to remain as his guest while he went next day to Seoul to look up Yi in West School Ward. He found him, and told him why he had come.

Yi said, "I already knew of this." So the two journeyed together to the inquirer's home.

When there, they went with the guest up the hill. Yi asked of the guest, "Why did you tell the master to change the site ?"

The guest replied, "This hill is a Kneeling Pheasant formation. If the pheasant kneels too long it cannot endure it, so that within a limited time it must fly. Ten years is the time; that's why I spoke."

Yi laughed and said, "Your idea is only a partial view, you have thought of only one thing, there are other conditions that enter." Then he showed the peak to the rear, and said, "Yonder is Dog Hill," and then one below, "which," said he, "is Falcon Hill," and then the stream in front, "which," said he, "is Cat River. This is the whole group, the dog behind, the falcon just above, and the cat in front, how then can the pheasant fly? It dares not."

The guest replied, "Teacher, surely your eyes are enlightened, and see further than those of ordinary men."

From that day forth the Yis of Pine Hill became a great and noted family.

Source: "The Geomancer," James S. Gale. *Korean Folk Tales: Imps, Ghosts and Fairies Translated from the Korean of Im Bang and Yi Ryuk.* (London: J.M. Dent & Sons, Ltd., 1913), pp. 69–72.

HEROES, HEROINES, TRICKSTERS, AND FOOLS

Momotaro: The Peach Boy

The tale of "Momotaro: The Peach Boy" is one of the most commonly retained traditional Japanese tales in the repertoires of Japanese Americans. Momotaro, who leads a successful quest against an island of murderous devils, exhibits the characteristics of monster-slayers cross-culturally. Strange circumstances attend his birth. He is physically precocious, and he uses his wits as well as his weapons. The Peach Boy not only has survived in traditional culture but has made the transition to contemporary children's popular literature and anthologies of Asian folktales (for example, Peach Boy *by Florence Sakade and Yoshisuke Kurosaki).*

Long, long ago there lived an old man and an old woman; they were peasants, and had to work hard to earn their daily rice. The old man used to go and cut grass for the farmers around, and while he was gone the old woman, his wife, did the work of the house and worked in their own little rice field.

One day the old man went to the hills as usual to cut grass and the old woman took some clothes to the river to wash.

It was nearly summer, and the country was very beautiful to see in its fresh greenness as the two old people went on their way to work. The grass on the hanks of the river looked like emerald velvet, and the pussy willows along the edge of the water were shaking out their soft tassels.

The breezes blew and ruffled the smooth surface of the water into wavelets, and passing on touched the cheeks of the old couple who, for some reason they could not explain, felt very happy that morning.

The old woman at last found a nice spot by the river bank and put her basket down. Then she set to work to wash the clothes; she took them one by one out of the basket and washed them in the river and rubbed them on the stones.

The water was as clear as crystal, and she could see the tiny fish swimming to and fro, and the pebbles at the bottom.

As she was busy washing her clothes a great peach came bumping down the stream. The old woman looked up from her work and saw this large peach. She was sixty years of age, yet in all her life she had never seen such a big peach as this.

"How delicious that peach must be!" she said to herself. "I must certainly get it and take it home to my old man."

She stretched out her arm to try and get it, but it was quite out of her reach. She looked about for a stick, but there was not one to be seen, and if she went to look for one she would lose the peach.

Stopping a moment to think what she would do, she remembered an old charm-verse. Now she began to clap her hands to keep time to the rolling of the peach down stream, and while she clapped she sang this song:

> "Distant water is bitter,
> The near water is sweet;
> Pass by the distant water
> And come into the sweet."

Strange to say, as soon as she began to repeat this little song the peach began to come nearer and nearer the bank where the old woman was standing, till at last it stopped just in front of her so that she was able to take it up in her hands.

The old woman was delighted. She could not go on with her work, so happy and excited was she, so she put all the clothes back in her bamboo basket, and with the basket on her back and the peach in her hand she hurried homewards.

It seemed a very long time to her to wait till her husband returned. The old man at last came back as the sun was setting, with a big bundle of grass on his back so big that he was almost hidden and she could hardly see him. He seemed very tired and used the scythe for a walking stick, leaning on it as he walked along.

As soon as the old woman saw him she called out, "Old Man! I have been waiting for you to come home for such a long time today!"

"What is the matter? Why are you so impatient?" asked the old man, wondering at her unusual eagerness. "Has anything happened while I have been away?"

"Oh, no!" answered the old woman, "nothing has happened, only I have found a nice present for you!"

"That is good," said the old man. He then washed his feet in a basin of water and stepped up to the veranda.

The old woman now ran into the little room and brought out from the cupboard the big peach. It felt even heavier than before. She held it up to him, saying, "Just look at this! Did you ever see such a large peach in all your life?"

When the old man looked at the peach he was greatly astonished and said, "This is indeed the largest peach I have ever seen! Wherever did you buy it?"

"I did not buy it," answered the old woman. "I found it in the river where I was washing."

And she told him the whole story.

"I am very glad that you have found it. Let us eat it now, for I am hungry," said the O Fii San. He brought out the kitchen knife, and, placing the peach on a board, was about to cut it when, wonderful to tell, the peach split in two of itself and a clear voice said: "Wait a bit, old man!" and out stepped a beautiful little child.

The old man and his wife were both so astonished at what they saw that they fell to the ground. The child spoke again: "Don't be afraid. I am no demon or fairy. I will tell you the truth. Heaven has had compassion on you. Every day and every night you have lamented that you had no child. Your cry has been heard and I am sent to be the son of your old age!"

On hearing this the old man and his wife were very happy. They had cried night and day for sorrow at having no child to help them in their lonely old age, and now that their prayer was answered they were so lost with joy that they did not know where to put their hands or their feet. First the old man took the child up in his arms, and then the old woman did the same; and they named him Momotaro, or Son of a Peach, because he had come out of a peach.

The years passed quickly by and the child grew to be fifteen years of age. He was taller and far stronger than any other boys of his own age, he had a handsome face and a heart full of courage, and he was very wise for his years. The old couple's pleasure was very great when they looked at him, for he was just what they thought a hero ought to be like.

One day Momotaro came to his foster-father and said solemnly: "Father, by a strange chance we have become father and son. Your goodness to me has been higher than the mountain grasses which it was your daily work to cut, and deeper than the river where my mother washes the clothes. I do not know how to thank you enough."

"Why," answered the old man, "it is a matter of course that a father should bring up his son. When you are older it will be your turn to take care of us, so after all there will be no profit or loss between us, all will be equal. Indeed, I am rather surprised that you should thank me in this way!" and the old man looked bothered.

"I hope you will be patient with me," said Momotaro, "but before I begin to pay back your goodness to me I have a request to make which I hope you will grant me above everything else."

"I will let you do whatever you wish, for you are quite different to all other boys!"

"Then let me go away at once!"

"What do you say? Do you wish to leave your old father and mother and go away from your old home?"

"I will surely come back again, if you let me go now!"

"Where are you going?"

"You must think it strange that I want to go away." said Momotaro, "because I have not yet told you my reason. Far away from here to the northeast of Japan there is an island in the sea. This island is the stronghold of a band of devils. I have often heard how they invade this land, kill and rob the people, and carry off all they can find. They are not only very wicked but they are disloyal to our Emperor and disobey his laws. They are also cannibals, for they kill and eat some of the poor people who are so unfortunate as to fall into their hands. These devils are very hateful beings. I must go and conquer them and bring back all the plunder of which they have robbed this land. It is for this reason that I want to go away for a short time!"

The old man was much surprised at hearing all this from a mere boy of fifteen. He thought it best to let the boy go. He was strong and fearless, and besides all this, the old man knew he was no common child, for he had been sent to them as a gift from Heaven, and he felt quite sure that the devils would be powerless to harm him.

"All you say is very interesting, Momotaro," said the old man. "I will not hinder you in your determination. You may go if you wish. Go to the island as soon as ever you like and destroy the demons and bring peace to the land."

"Thank you for all your kindness," said Momotaro, who began to get ready to go that very day. He was full of courage and did not know what fear was.

The old man and woman at once set to work to pound rice in the kitchen mortar to make cakes for Momotaro to take with him on his journey. At last the cakes were made and Momotaro was ready to start on his long journey.

Parting is always sad. So it was now. The eyes of the two old people were filled with tears and their voices trembled as they said: "Go with all care and speed. We expect you back victorious!"

Momotaro was very sorry to leave his old parents (though he knew he was coming back as soon as he could), for he thought of how lonely they would be while he was away. But he said "Good-by!" quite bravely.

"I am going now. Take good care of yourselves while I am away. Good-by!" And he stepped quickly out of the house. In silence the eyes of Momotaro and his parents met in farewell."

Momotaro now hurried on his way till it was midday. He began to feel hungry, so he opened his bag and took out one of the rice-cakes and sat down under a tree by the side of the road to eat it. While he was thus having his lunch a dog almost as large as a colt came running out from the high grass. He made straight for Momotaro, and showing his teeth, said in a fierce way: "You are a rude man to pass my field without asking permission first. If you leave me all the cakes you have in your bag you may go; otherwise I will bite you till I kill you!"

Momotaro only laughed scornfully: "What is that you are saying? Do you know who I am? I am Momotaro, and I am on my way to subdue the devils in their island stronghold in the northeast of Japan. If you try to stop me on my way there I will cut you in two from the head downwards!"

The dog's manner at once changed. His tail dropped between his legs, and coming near he bowed so low that his forehead touched the ground. "What do I hear? The name of Momotaro! Are you indeed Momotaro? I have often heard of your great strength. Not knowing who you were I have behaved in a very stupid way. Will you please pardon my rudeness? Are you indeed on your way to invade the Island of Devils? If you will take such a rude fellow with you as one of your followers, I shall be very grateful to you."

"I think I can take you with me if you wish to go," said Momotaro.

"Thank you!" said the dog. "By the way, I am very, very hungry. Will you give me one of the cakes you are carrying?"

"This is the best kind of cake there is in Japan," said Momotaro. "I cannot spare you a whole one; I will give you half of one."

"Thank you very much," said the dog, taking the piece thrown to him.

Then Momotaro got up and the dog followed. For a long time they walked over the hills and through the valleys. As they were going along an animal came down from a tree a little ahead of them. The creature soon came up to Momotaro and said: "Good morning, Momotaro! You are welcome in this part of the country. Will you allow me to go with you?"

The dog answered jealously, "Momotaro already has a dog to accompany him. Of what use is a monkey like you in battle? We are on our way to fight the devils! Get away!"

The dog and the monkey began to quarrel and bite, for these two animals always hate each other.

"Now, don't quarrel!" said Momotaro, putting himself between them. "Wait a moment, dog!"

"It is not at all dignified for you to have such a creature as that following you!" said the dog.

"What do you know about it?" asked Momotaro; and pushing aside the dog, he spoke to the monkey "Who are you?"

"I am a monkey living in these hills," replied the monkey. "I heard of your expedition to the Island of Devils, and I have come to go with you. Nothing will please me more than to follow you!"

"Do you really wish to go to the Island of Devils and fight with me?"

"Yes, sir," replied the monkey.

"I admire your courage," said Momotaro. "Here is a piece of one of my fine rice-cakes. Come along!"

So the monkey joined Momotaro. The dog and the monkey did not get on well together. They were always snapping at each other as they went along, and always wanting to have a fight. This made Momotaro very cross, and at last he sent the dog on ahead with a flag and put the monkey behind with a sword, and he placed himself between them with a war-fan, which is made of iron.

By and by they came to a large field. Here a bird flew down and alighted on the ground just in front of the little party. It was the most beautiful bird Momotaro had ever seen. On its body were five different robes of feathers and its head was covered with a scarlet cap.

The dog at once ran at the bird and tried to seize and kill it. But the bird struck out its spurs and flew at the dog's tail, and the fight went hard with both.

Momotaro, as he looked on, could not help admiring the bird; it showed so much spirit in the fight. It would certainly make a good fighter. Momotaro went up to the two combatants, and holding the dog back, said to the bird: "You rascal! You are hindering my journey. Surrender at once, and I will take you with me. If you don't I will set this dog to bite your head off!"

Then the bird surrendered at once, and begged to be taken into Momotaro's company. "I do not know what excuse to offer for quarreling with the dog, your servant, but I did not see you. I am a miserable bird called a pheasant. It is very generous of you to pardon my rudeness and to take me with you. Please allow me to follow you behind the dog and the monkey!"

"I congratulate you on surrendering so soon," said Momotaro, smiling. "Come and join us in our raid on the devils."

"Are you going to take this bird with you also?" asked the dog, interrupting.

"Why do you ask such an unnecessary question? Didn't you hear what I said? I take the bird with me because I wish to!"

"Humph!" said the dog.

Then Momotaro stood and gave this order, "Now all of you must listen to me. The first thing necessary in an army is harmony. It is a wise saying which says that 'Advantage on earth is better than advantage in heaven!' Union amongst ourselves is better than any earthly gain. When we are not at peace amongst ourselves it is no easy thing to subdue an enemy. From now, you three, the dog, the monkey and the pheasant, must be friends with one mind. The one who first begins a quarrel will be discharged on the spot!"

All the three promised not to quarrel. The pheasant was now made a member of Momotaro's suite, and received half a cake.

Momotaro's influence was so great that the three became good friends, and hurried onwards with him as their leader.

Hurrying on day after day they at last came out upon the shore of the North-Eastern Sea. There was nothing to be seen as far as the horizon not a sign of any island. All that broke the stillness was the rolling of the waves upon the shore.

Now, the dog and the monkey and the pheasant had come very bravely all the way through the long valleys and over the hills, but they had never seen the sea before, and for the first time since they set out they were bewildered and gazed at each other in silence. How were they to cross the water and get to the Island of Devils? Momotaro soon saw that they were daunted by the sight of the sea, and to try them he spoke loudly and roughly: "Why do you hesitate? Are you afraid of the sea? Oh! What cowards you are! It is impossible to take such weak creatures as you with me to fight the demons. It will be far better for me to go alone. I discharge you all at once!"

The three animals were taken aback at this sharp reproof, and clung to Momotaro's sleeve, begging him not to send them away.

"Please, Momotaro!" said the dog.

"We have come thus far!" said the monkey.

"It is inhuman to leave us here!" said the pheasant.

"We are not at all afraid of the sea," said the monkey again.

"Please do take us with you," said the pheasant.

"Do please," said the dog.

They had now gained a little courage, so Momotaro said, "Well, then, I will take you with me, but be careful!"

Momotaro now got a small ship, and they all got on board. The wind and weather were fair, and the ship went like an arrow over the sea. It was the first time they had ever been on the water, and so at first the dog, the monkey and the pheasant were frightened at the waves and the rolling of the vessel, but by degrees they grew accustomed to the water and were quite happy again. Every day they paced the deck of their little ship, eagerly looking out for the demons island.

When they grew tired of this, they told each other stories of all their exploits of which they were proud, and then played games together; and Momotaro found much to amuse him in listening to the three animals and watching their antics, and in this way he forgot that the way was long and that he was tired of the voyage and of doing nothing. He longed to be at work killing the monsters who had done so much harm in his country.

As the wind blew in their favor and they met no storms the ship made a quick voyage, and one day when the sun was shining brightly a sight of land rewarded the four watchers at the bow.

Momotaro knew at once that what they saw was the devils' stronghold. On the top of the precipitous shore, looking out to sea, was a large castle. Now that his enterprise was close at hand, he was deep in thought with his head leaning on his hands, wondering how he should begin the attack.

His three followers watched him, waiting for orders. At last he called to the pheasant: "It is a great advantage for us to have you with us," said Momotaro to the bird, "for you have good wings. Fly at once to the castle and engage the demons to fight. We will follow you."

The pheasant at once obeyed. He flew off from the ship beating the air gladly with his wings, The bird soon reached the island and took up his position on the roof in the middle of the castle, calling out loudly: "All you devils listen to me! The great Japanese general Momotaro has come to fight you and to take your stronghold from you. If you wish to save your lives surrender at once, and in token of your submission you must break off the horns that grow on your forehead. If you do not surrender at once, but make up your mind to fight, we, the pheasant, the dog and the monkey, will kill you all by biting and tearing you to death!"

The horned demons looking up and only seeing a pheasant, laughed and said: "A wild pheasant, indeed! It is ridiculous to hear such words from a mean thing like you. Wait till you get a blow from one of our iron bars!"

Very angry, indeed, were the devils. They shook their horns and their shocks of red hair fiercely, and rushed to put on tiger skin trousers to make themselves look more terrible. They then brought out great iron bars and ran to where the pheasant perched over their heads, and tried to knock him down. The pheasant flew to one side to escape the blow, and then attacked the head of first one and then another demon. He flew round and round them, beating the air with his wings so fiercely and ceaselessly, that the devils began to wonder whether they had to fight one or many more birds.

In the meantime, Momotaro had brought his ship to land. As they had approached, he saw that the shore was like a precipice, and that the large castle was surrounded by high walls and large iron gates and was strongly fortified.

Momotaro landed, and with the hope of finding some way of entrance, walked up the path towards the top, followed by the monkey and the dog. They soon came upon two beautiful damsels washing clothes in a stream. Momotaro saw that the clothes were blood-stained, and that as the two maidens washed, the tears were falling fast down their cheeks. He stopped and spoke to them: "Who are you, and why do you weep?"

"We are captives of the Demon King. We were carried away from our homes to this island, and though we are the daughters of Daimios (Lords), we are obliged to be his servants, and one day he will kill us" and the maidens held up the blood-stained clothes "and eat us, and there is no one to help us!"

And their tears burst out afresh at this horrible thought.

"I will rescue you," said Momotaro. "Do not weep any more, only show me how I may get into the castle."

Then the two ladies led the way and showed Momotaro a little back door in the lowest part of the castle wall so small that Momotaro could hardly crawl in.

The pheasant, who was all this time fighting hard, saw Momotaro and his little band rush in at the back. Momotaro's onslaught was so furious that the devils could not stand against him. At first their foe had been a single bird, the pheasant, but now that Momotaro and the dog and the monkey had arrived they were bewildered, for the four enemies fought like a hundred, so strong were they. Some of the devils fell off the parapet of the castle and were dashed to pieces on the rocks beneath; others fell into the sea and were drowned; many were beaten to death by the three animals.

The chief of the devils at last was the only one left. He made up his mind to surrender, for he knew that his enemy was stronger than mortal man. He came up humbly to Momotaro and threw down his iron bar, and kneeling down at the victor's feet he broke off the horns on his head in token of submission, for they were the sign of his strength and power.

"I am afraid of you," he said meekly. "I cannot stand against you. I will give you all the treasure hidden in this castle if you will spare my life!"

Momotaro laughed. "It is not like you, big devil, to beg for mercy, is it? I cannot spare your wicked life, however much you beg, for you have killed and tortured many people and robbed our country for many years." Then Momotaro tied the devil chief up and gave him into the monkey's charge. Having done this, he went into all the rooms of the castle and set the prisoners free and gathered together all the treasure he found.

The dog and the pheasant carried home the plunder, and thus Momotaro returned triumphantly to his home, taking with him the devil chief as a captive.

The two poor damsels, daughters of Daimios ["daimyo", feudal lord] and others whom the wicked demon had carried off to be his slaves, were taken safely to their own homes and delivered to their parents. The whole country made a hero of Momotaro on his triumphant return, and rejoiced that the country was now freed from the robber devils who had been a terror of the land for a long time.

The old couple's joy was greater than ever, and the treasure Momotaro had brought home with him enabled them to live in peace and plenty to the end of their days.

Source: "Momotaro," Yei Theodora Ozaki. *Japanese Fairy Tales.* (New York: Grosset and Dunlap, 1906), pp. 251–270.

Monkey King: A Record of a Journey to the Western Paradise to Procure the Buddhist Scriptures for the Emperor of China

The narrative of T'ang Sung's pilgrimage to obtain the Buddhist scriptures is likely to be the best-known Chinese traditional narrative in the world. For Buddhists it is in many ways the equivalent of John Bunyan's The Pilgrim's Progress *for Christians. T'ang Sung is said to symbolize conscience. Monkey, Sun Hou, symbolizes human nature, prone to weakness, temptation, and evil. The Pig, Chu Pa-chieh, often described as bearing a muckrake although he carries a gun in this version, is the embodiment of coarser human passions. The Foolish Priest, Sha Ho-shang, Priest Sha, is interpreted as a human character, weak and in need of support and encouragement. Kwan-yin (see "The Princess Kwan-yin," p. 3) plays an important role in the tale. This popular story has been retold in various forms for over 400 years. In 2008,* The Forbidden Kingdom, *a film based on the "Monkey King:..." was released, featuring action stars Jackie Chan and Jet Li.*

In the year 629 A.D., a very devout monk, T'ang Sung, hoping to achieve merit by which he might avoid death and that he might become one of the Eternal Holy Ones, accepted the proposal of his Emperor that he should go to the west in search of the famous Buddhist Classics.

Alone he set out on his journey to the Yellow River where the caravans to India were wont to form. On his way he met a wonderful monkey. The monkey asked the priest where he was going, and on being told, decided that he would go along with the good priest. "But what can you do? Why should you go?" asked the monk.

The monkey replied, "I am a famous jumper. With one jump I can touch the heavens; I can walk on water and on the air; I can change myself into seventy-two different shapes." After some more conversation the monk consented to the company of the monkey, and giving him the name Sun Hou, he fastened a string to his neck and started on his way.

The monkey was very changeful in his disposition and the monk had a hard time making him mind.

After going a few miles he met a holy man who said, "If he does not mind you I will tell you something to say to him which will make his head ache, and he will go quietly with you."

Going along a few more miles they met a pig, and on hearing from the monkey where they were going, said he also would go and help find the books.

"What can you do to help?" asked T'ang Sung.

"I can catch thieves and have power to do many strange things," was the reply; "and the only trouble with me is that I walk slowly."

The monk considered the question, and as he did not like to be unkind to a pig said he could go. Afterward on the road they met a very stupid simple priest, and he pled so hard to be allowed to join the party that the monk also consented; thus the four traveled slowly along until they met a white horse.

He asked the errand of the strange company, and after hearing the story, said he also would go and T'ang Sung might ride him. The foolish priest carried the baggage, the pig carried the gun, and the monkey was sent on ahead to make all the arrangements.

On the road to India they had to pass seventy-two caves, where demons lived, who were ever on the watch for travelers.

One day they traveled till night; all day they had been without food, and as darkness came on and no village was in sight the monkey said, "I will jump and see where a village is." He gave a great jump and saw they were not far from a village; he heard a great noise which frightened him; he gave another jump and saw the village was on the bank of a great river eight hundred yards wide. The monkey returned and got his companions and led them to the home of the rich man of the village.

He struck the bell the priest carried, and the servants, on opening the gate and seeing the queer procession, were very much frightened. Sun Hou said, "Don't be afraid. We are from the Emperor, and going to India to get the sacred books of the great Buddha. We want something to eat and a place to sleep, as we are very weary."

The owner of the place replied, "I am able to give what you ask, but not tonight as I am in great trouble."

"What is it? Perhaps I can help you," said the monkey.

Then said the rich man, "For long years a terrible demon has lived in the river and every year we have to prepare a young boy and a young girl as an offering for him or he will destroy the village by causing the river to overflow. Tonight is the yearly sacrifice and it falls on me. I am a large householder, but I have only one little boy and one little girl, and my heart is breaking with my grief, but I must give them up to save the lives of the many in the village."

Sun Hou said, after a moment's thought, "Don't be anxious. I have a plan. Get us something to eat."

After eating, Sun Hou commanded that the children should be brought into the room. After looking at them Sun Hou said to the pig, "You impersonate the girl and I will the boy."

The pig shook himself three times, and the father said, "Well done."

Soon after the procession, which had been forming in the village, came for them, with drums beating and banners flying. They carried the supposed children to the temple on the river bank. Cooked chicken was placed on the table, the incense lighted, then all went out and the door was locked.

Then when all was quiet Sun Hou said to the pig, "You take one side and I will the other and don't be afraid."

About midnight there was the sound of a great wind, and then Sun Hou said, "Be careful, the demon, Yao Ching, is coming."

Immediately the door opened and a great fishlike being came into the temple. They heard him say, "In the past I have taken the boy first, but tonight I shall eat the girl first." With that he seized the girl, who immediately struck him, and then, with the help of the boy, fought a terrible battle and injured him so that he fled, leaving two great fins on the floor.

The river-demon sought out the king of the demons and told him the story. He said, "You call up a great cold wind, bring snow and ice and freeze over the river, then when they get half-way over the river, you call your friends to help you and put your strength together and cause the ice to give way and precipitate them all into the river."

The demon was pleased with the plan and in three days the ice was so thick that farmers could cross in their carts. All this time the four strange companions were living in great comfort with the rich man of the house, who gave them many rich presents and much food.

On the fourth day they started on, and when they got to the middle of the river the ice broke and all went into the water except the monkey, who gave a great jump and landed on the top of a high mountain. The others were taken captive, and put in a deep cave by the river-demon to wait until they had caught Sun Hou, when all should be eaten together.

Day after day, Sun Hou went down on the river bank and reviled them. Many were the fierce battles they fought but neither could get the victory. At last one day Sun Hou took a mighty jump and arrived at the home of the Goddess of Mercy, who was in her palace in the Southern Sea.

"Ah!" said she; "I knew you were coming. I have waited for you." She was making a fish basket of bamboo. When she heard his troubles she said, "Wait. I am making this great fish-basket to catch him in. He used to live in my sea, and is my special food fish, but he rebelled and ran away and for many years has lived in the great river. You go back and call him and fight again, and I will come and get him in my basket." In the terrible battle which followed the Goddess of Mercy let from Heaven a basket and took him in and up to Heaven.

Then Sun Hou called some of the Heavenly Soldiers to his aid, and they went with him and found his companions in a cave, but alas the men could not swim. While Sun Hou was pondering, a big turtle came along and said, "I knock [bow] my head to you. You are my preserver. Many years ago this cave was mine, but the river-demons took it, and now, to show my thanks, if you will all get on my back I will carry you over the river."

This they did, and on the way the turtle said, "You are going to India to find out how one can live forever? Will you ask the merciful Buddha what my afterlife is to be like?"

Sun Hou promised, and as they would need help in crossing on their return he was to look out for them.

As they traveled on they came to the country of Pii Tao. The king asked them where they were going and also demanded a proof of their Imperial mission. Now, this king had three famous ministers called Fox, Deer, and Sheep. They said these persons must first prove their strength before they could go on their way. To the question as to whether their contest was to be of military skill or a contest of mind, the monkey chose the latter.

A platform thirty feet high was built. Then Minister Fox said to T'ang Sung, "We two will go up there and see which can sit without moving an eyelash for the longest time; the one who moves first is to be killed."

While thus sitting the sheep changed himself into a worm and crawled up on the bald head of the priest, and bit his head in many places. T'ang Sung was most uncomfortable and his face showed it.

Now, Sun Hou saw the look and so changed himself into a bird, flew up over the monk, and seeing the worm, flew down and in picking it up saw that it was the "Minister Sheep," to whom he said, "If this is the trick I will show you what I can do," and changed himself into a centipede, and crawled upon Minister Fox. He entered his nose, got into his ear, and up into his head, and so distracted did the minister become that he could not endure the pain, and threw himself from the platform and thus died.

When the "Minister Deer" saw the calamity he said, "Our great elder brother is dead, I will see what I can do," so he said, "Let us see who can cut his head off, throw it away, get it again and grow it on."

Sun Hou said, "That is good. It is not the monk's turn; this is my turn."

Minister Deer asked, "Who will try first, you or I?"

Sun Hou replied, "I can cut my head off and grow it on again ten times."

The Deer replied, "I can only once."

So Sun Hou said, "I will try first," and immediately cut off his head, upon which Minister Deer said, "I can only cut mine off once and I won't do it now."

"If you don't, we will fight," said Sun Hou.

Thus driven, he cut his head off, and the monkey, changing to a dog, ran away with it and was gone two hours, so long that the Deer died also.

Then said Minister Sheep, "You must conquer me or I shall kill you."

"Well," said Sun Hou, "what shall we do? You decide."

"Well," said the Sheep, "we will build a fire, put on a big kettle of oil, and when it boils we will take turns in getting in and staying two hours. The one who can do it will be the victor."

So all was ready and Sun Hou got in; before getting in he repeated a charm to the dragon, who came and changed him into a nail and kept the oil in the bottom of the kettle cold while it boiled on top.

After two hours Minister Sheep said, "He is dead," and getting a skimmer he felt around and brought out a nail, which changed to a man, saying, "Ah, I was asleep; having such a good rest. Now it is your turn and I shall not sleep any more."

Thus the Minister Sheep was obliged to get in.

Then Sun Hou called the king and said to him, "Look at your great ministers; how can you expect the country to grow and improve when your three greatest ministers are such demons? See what frauds they are, and how they impose on you and the people."

To this the king replied, "I see you are great men and wonderful. You cannot go yet; it is a famine year and you must call down rain for us."

Sun Hou said, "I will go to Heaven and plead with the great Lord of the Heaven."

With a jump he was in Heaven; to his petition the great God said, "There is no rain for Tibet for three years." After much pleading from Sun Hou the God replied, "I will give you two inches only."

When the king heard this he said, "That is not enough, I must have more. If you can get two inches you can get more, and then I will let you go."

So Sun Hou said, "I will get you two feet."

"That is too much," replied the king, "but a little more than we need is no great matter, only get it."

When Sun Hou told the great God of Rain, he said, "I will not let them say how much I am to give, I will give enough."

When Sun Hou took this message to the king he thanked them and let them go on their way, promising to entertain them on their return.

They went on their journey; the monk, T'ang Sung, riding the white horse, the priest praying and reading. At night they came to the foot of a high mountain where there was a temple where lived a demon. This temple was called the "Temple of Thunder." Sun Hou told the priest he did not think the temple was safe, but the priest said it must be because it was a temple, and he was sure they would find rest and food. When they saw the name of the temple they bowed their heads and went slowly forward until they saw what seemed a great image of Buddha.

When Sun Hou came close to it he said, "That is not the Buddha," and refused to bow his head.

Just then a voice said, "Why do you not bow your head?" to which Sun Hou replied, "I do not think you look like Buddha."

Immediately they heard a bell strike and something was let down from above and enveloped them in darkness. Sun Hou felt of it; it was hard like copper. They walked all around it but could not get out. They exerted all their combined strength but could not remove the darkness.

Then Sun Hou repeated his wonderful charm and twenty-eight soldiers from the great lord of the Heaven suddenly came in the shape of a great cow. Sun Hou called to him to make a hole with his horn; this he did, but when he pulled out his horn the hole closed up; again he did it, and Sun Hou changed into a mustard seed and was pulled out by the cow.

Then he let the soldiers out of the iron cow and the great demon got a great string and bound them and put them in a cave. Sun Hou gradually grew smaller and his rope loosened and he escaped; with one jump he reached Heaven and brought down many soldiers from the great God.

When the great demon saw them he said, "I am not afraid of you, even if you are from Heaven. I will yet eat you."

Among the Heavenly Soldiers was one very great one, and he wore a wheel of iron on one foot and a wheel of wind on the other; on his wrist was a beautiful bracelet and he wore a Heavenly chain. A terrible battle was fought in the air between the soldiers of the demons and the Heavenly band. The great demon threw up his charmed lasso and brought down the bracelet, and again, and brought down the chain.

Then Sun Hou saw him lasso all the Heavenly Soldiers, and just as the string was to envelope him he gave a jump and turned a somersault and landed on top of a mountain. There he gave himself up to despair in a cave. Along came a man who asked why he was crying and he said, "I promised to take a monk to India and to protect him. He and his companions are bound and in a cave. I got twenty-eight servants from the great God, they are also bound; and now all the Heavenly Soldiers have been defeated and are bound."

"You are too impatient," replied the man. "Do you not remember that a great iron beam can be rubbed to a fine needle if you but take time? You go to the demons who live in these caves in the mountains, and find out what kind of a demon this is."

Sun Hou went to them all and at last found one who said he knew the demon of the Thunder temple. He had one time been his servant but had stolen his treasure and run away. "You can only take him by craft and I will help you. He is most fond of melons, and we will plant some melons and test him. I will be the gardener and you go and call him out."

Then Sun Hou went out and reviled the demon and he came out in great anger; Sun Hou changed into a fine melon and the demon, seeing him, ate him. Sun Hou said, "Now I will tear your heart out of you."

In his great distress the demon pleaded so hard that Sun Hou came out by the demon's ear and together they fought all over the melon patch in the moonlight. After the battle, worn and weary, Sun Hou liberated the soldiers and his companions, and then looking about him saw there was no mountain, no temple, but a fine restful road with eating-houses and rest-houses on the way.

"Ah, monk," said he, "so it ever is with earth's power and glory. It is all vanity, vanity empty, empty."

In restful travel they reached their journey's end and found the book. On their return journey they had many adventures, but they had all grown wiser and learned much.

Source: Adapted from "T'ang Sung's Journey to Get the Buddhist Classics," Nellie N. Russell. *Gleanings from Chinese Folklore.* (New York: Fleming H. Revell, 1915), pp. 110–123.

The Fish Prince

This classic South Asian tale bears many similarities to the complex European folktales familiar to most Americans. The motifs of the enchanted prince in animal form, the helpful animals, and the wickedness motivated by jealousy are shared in common throughout the Indo-European folktale repertoire and allow tales of this sort to remain viable in new contexts. Ties to traditional Hindu culture are evident in elements such as the fakir (a Hindu ascetic and magician) references to the saree (usually spelled, "sari," the traditional Indian woman's outer garment).

There were once a Rajah and Ranee who had no child, though every day they prayed that one might be sent to them. For this reason the Ranee at last became quite melancholy, and took no more pleasure in anything.

One day some fish were brought to the palace kitchen to be prepared as usual for the Rajah's dinner. Among them was one such as the cook had never seen before. Its scales shone with all the colors of the rainbow, and upon its head was a mark that looked like a little golden crown. The cook examined it curiously, and then was about to prepare it for cooking as he had done with the others, but it lifted up its head and spoke to him.

"Do not kill me," said the fish. " Instead, put me in a basin of water and carry mc to the Ranee, and it may be I will amuse her."

The cook was very much surprised to hear a fish speaking, and it seemed to him such a wonderful creature that it might very well amuse even the Ranee; he therefore put it in a basin of water, and gave it to a maid, and bade her carry it to the queen.

The maid did as she was told, and the Ranee was indeed very much pleased with the beautiful little fish. All day she kept it beside her and watched its quick movements and its changing colors. The next day she was even more pleased with it, and before long she became so fond of it that she could not have loved it better if it had been her own child. She named it Muchie Rajah, or the Fish Prince, and called it her son.

After a time the fish grew so large that it could no longer live in the basin, and then it was put in a marble bath. As it still continued to grow, the Ranee had a great tank made for it out in the palace gardens. Here every day she went to visit it. She always carried some rice with her, and when she called it, the great fish would rise through the water and eat from her hand, and play about where she could see it.

But one day when the Ranee came to the tank she saw Muchie Rajah lying on the water very still. His colors looked dull, and when she called to him he came to her slowly, and would not eat the rice she had brought to him.

The Ranee was greatly troubled. "Alas, my dear son," she cried, "what is it that ails you? Are you sick, that you will not eat the good rice I have brought to you?"

"I am not sick" answered the great fish, "but I am very, very lonely. My mother, I beg of you to have a little room built in the side of the tank, and bring some young girl to live in it all the time and be company for me."

The Ranee could refuse nothing to her dear Muchie Rajah. She immediately sent for masons and stone-cutters, and had a little room made in the side of the tank. The room was so cleverly built that the fish could reach his head over the side of it, and yet it was protected from the water in such a way that one could live in it safely and not be drowned. The walls of it were carved and colored and set with precious stones, so that it was very beautiful, and there were hanging lamps in it to give light by day and night.

After all was finished, the Ranee sent out messengers through the country to find some beautiful girl to come and live in the little room, and be the bride of her dear Muchie Rajah. To the parents of such a girl she promised to give a bag of gold.

But though the messengers journeyed far and near, they could find no parents who were willing to give their daughter to the Fish Prince. "No, no," they said; "our daughters are worth more to us than a bag of gold. This Muchie Rajah is very large and strong and fierce, and what he wishes is not a bride, but some young girl to eat."

Now not far from the palace there lived a fakir, whose wife had died and left him with one daughter. This girl, whose name was Balna, was very beautiful. After the death of his first wife the fakir married again. The second wife also had a daughter, but her daughter was as ugly as Balna was beautiful, and as ill-tempered as Balna was sweet and gentle.

The stepmother hated Balna and was very jealous of her, and would have done anything to rid the house of her.

One time the fakir went away on a long journey, leaving his house and all that was in it in the charge of his wife. The messengers were still seeking for a bride for the Muchie Rajah, and as soon as the fakir had gone his wife sent for them, and said, " I have a daughter whom I am willing to let you have for the Fish Prince, and as she is very beautiful I am sure you will be delighted with her."

The messengers were very glad to hear this, and said they would come for the girl the next day, and bring a bag of gold to the woman in payment for her.

After they had gone the stepmother called Balna to her and told her what she had promised.

The girl was very much frightened. "Alas!" she cried, "what have you done? The great fish will certainly eat me. If my father had been here he would never have allowed you to sell me."

"This is silly talk," answered the stepmother.

"Why should the fish eat you? He is lonely and wishes a companion. You ought to be proud and happy to be the wife of a Rajah, even if he is only a fish."

She then bade the girl go down to the river and wash her saree, that she might be clean and neat when the messengers came for her.

Balna took her saree and went down to the river to wash it, and as she washed it she wept bitterly.

Now it so happened that an old seven-headed cobra had a hole in the bank of the river, and lived there with his wife and children. He heard the sound of weeping just above him, and it kept on for so long that after a while he stuck one of his heads out of the hole and spoke to the girl.

"Why are you weeping here?" he said. "Do you not know that your tears are dropping down into my house like rain, and that they are very salt?"

"Oh, Father Cobra, excuse me," answered the girl, "but I have good cause to weep. My stepmother has sold me to be the bride of Muchie Rajah, and I know he will certainly eat me, for he is very large and fierce."

"Listen to me, daughter," said the cobra, "for I am very wise and know all things. This great fish you speak of is not a fish at all, but the Rajah of a far country. In some way he offended the gods, and as a punishment he was changed into the shape of a fish and sent to live in the river.

Now if you will do exactly what I tell you to do, you can break this enchantment and become his Ranee; but if you do not do as I say, then he will of a certainty eat you as you fear."

The cobra then gave the girl three stones, and bade her tie them into the corner of her saree so as not to lose them. "Tomorrow the messengers will come and take you to Muchie Rajah," he said. "They will put you in the little room in the side of the tank. When it is night, you must not on any account go to sleep. If you do, you will be lost. But take these stones in your hand and watch. When he comes near you, throw a stone at him. Immediately he will sink to the bottom of the tank and will lie there for a while. When he comes again, throw the second stone at him and he will again go away, and when he comes for the third time, throw the third stone. Then the enchantment will be broken, and he will resume his natural form, and you will have nothing more to fear from him."

The girl heard with joy what the cobra said to her. She thanked him and tied the stones in the corner of the saree, and then she ran on home again. When she went into the house her stepmother was surprised to see how cheerful she had become. She no longer wept nor complained, and when, the next day, the messengers came for her, she was quite willing to go away with them.

At the palace the old Ranee was waiting impatiently for the bride, and she was delighted when she saw what a beautiful girl the messengers had brought with them.

Balna was taken out to the tank, and a great crowd of people followed to see what would become of her. Many of them pitied her, and they wondered that she went so cheerfully, for they expected no less than that she would be eaten by the great fish.

After she was put in the little room in the side of the tank the crowd waited about for a long time. Every moment they expected to see Muchie Rajah rise through the water and swallow her, but nothing happened. The water lay black and still, and there was no sound but the lapping of the little waves against the stonework.

After a while night came, and the people grew tired of waiting and went away to their homes. Balna was left in the little room all alone. She untied the corner of her saree and took out the three stones. Two she laid on the floor beside her, and one she kept in her hand.

About midnight the water was disturbed. The waves dashed louder against the stones. There was a hissing sound, and Muchie Rajah rose through the water. He came rushing on toward the room, his mouth open, and his scales as red as rubies.

Bahia was terribly frightened, but she held the stone fast and waited. When he was almost near enough to seize her, she threw the stone at him.

Immediately Muchie Rajah closed his jaws and sank down into the depths of the water where she could not see him.

After that she waited and watched for some time, but all was still. Then again the waves dashed louder. They rose to the edge of the stonework. Muchie Rajah came rushing through the water again, his mouth open, and his scales shining like fire.

Balna was more frightened than ever, but she threw the second stone at him, and again he sank through the water, and all was still.

This time he was gone longer than before, and the girl watched and waited. Then, suddenly, with a roaring sound, he came rushing at her again; his tail beat the waters into foam about him; his scales shone so red that the whole tank seemed full of blood.

Balna was almost dead with fright, but she managed to throw the third stone at him. No sooner did it touch Muchie Rajah than the enchantment was broken. Instead of the great fish, a handsome young Rajah stood there before her. He was dressed in cloth of gold embroidered in wonderful colors. His turban was fastened with an enormous ruby, and on his breast hung a chain set with precious stones. He took Balna by the hand and spoke to her.

"You have saved both my life and your own," he said. "The enchantment is broken, and now we can live together happily, and you and you only shall be my bride."

Very early the next morning the Ranee and her attendants came out to the tank to see whether the girl was still alive, or whether she had been eaten by the great fish. What was their surprise to find in the tank room not only Balna, but a handsome young prince, who told them he was Muchie Rajah. He also told them how Balna had broken the enchantment, and that now he would marry her and live in his own proper shape for ever.

Then there was great rejoicing, and the old Rajah and Ranee adopted the Fish Prince as their own son, and Balna was to them in place of a daughter.

When the fakir's wife heard what had happened to Balna, and how, instead of being eaten by the fish, she had become the bride of a great Rajah, she was ready to die with rage and spite. However, she hid her feelings and went to the palace and made friends with Balna. She pretended that she had only wished her well, and had known all along how it would turn out. Balna, who was very simple and forgiving, believed all the wicked stepmother said to her. She made her and the stepsister welcome at the palace, and gave them many gifts, but they only hated her more and more and were always plotting how they could injure her.

One time Balna and her stepmother and her stepsister went down to walk by the river in the cool of the afternoon. Presently the stepsister began to admire the young Ranee's jewels, and she asked Balna to let her try them on: "For," said she, "I have never worn such beautiful jewels as those are."

Balna was quite willing, and she took off the jewels and put them upon her sister the armlets, the necklaces, the rings, and the bracelets. Just at the last the stepsister allowed one of the earrings to fall to the ground. "Look," cried she, "I have dropped an earring. Do you pick it up for me, Balna, for I fear that if I stoop others may fall off too."

The young Ranee stooped for the earring. Then the stepmother gave her such a push that she fell into the river. The place where she fell in was very deep, and she sank out of sight immediately.

The two wicked women waited there for a while, but they saw nothing of her, so they were sure she must be drowned; then they went back to the palace.

The stepsister was still wearing all of Balna's jewels, and she was so covered up with them that every one thought she was the young Ranee. They went at once to Balna's apartments, and there the fakir's wife put her daughter to bed, and gave out that the Ranee was very ill and could see no one. It was a long time before even Muchie Rajah himself was allowed to enter the room. When he did, he was shocked to see how his beautiful bride had changed.

"It is because of her illness," said the fakir's wife. "Wait until she is well again, then all will be as it was before."

The young Rajah never doubted but that it was his bride who lay there, and he was very unhappy because his delicate Ranee had become so coarse and ugly and stupid. Still he was kind to her, and often came to visit her in her apartments.

But Balna had not been drowned as her stepmother and her sister thought. It so happened that the place where she had fallen into the river was close to where the old seven-headed cobra had his hole. He had heard the sound of voices overhead, and then a great splash; he looked out to see what had caused it, and there he saw the young Ranee struggling in the water. He felt sorry for her, and reached out and drew her into his hole. Then he carried her up to where she could get some air, for his hole had two openings, one into the river and one out on to the bank overhead.

The young Ranee was almost drowned, but presently she came to herself again. Then she wished to set out for the palace, but this the cobra would not allow her to do.

"Your stepmother and your sister are there even now," he said, "and if you went back they would certainly do you some harm. Stay here with me, and if your husband, the Rajah, comes to look for you, I will let you go back with him, but not otherwise."

When Balna heard this she was very sad, but she was obliged to stay there in the cobra's hole, as he said. After a time her little son was born there, and she named him Muchie Lai, the Ruby Fish, after his father.

The little Muchie Lai grew up strong and straight and handsome, and the old cobra became so fond of him that he loved him better than he did his own children; there was scarcely anything he would refuse him.

One day a bangle-seller came past the cobra's hole, and Muchie Lai wished to buy some of his bangles, but the cobra said, "No, these are very common bangles, and not suitable for a prince to wear. I will give the man some jewels, and he shall make for you bangles such as you ought to have."

The cobra then brought from his treasure house a number of diamonds and rubies and other precious stones. He gave them to the bangle-seller. "Take these," he said, "and make them into bangles, and bring them back to me as quickly as possible and you shall be well paid. And remember, they must be very handsome, for they are for this prince, Muchie Lai."

The bangle-seller took the stones home with him and made the bangles, and they were finished in a week's time. Then he started out to carry them back to the cobra. They were very handsome, and he was so proud of them that he carried them so that every one might see.

Now on his way it so chanced that he met Muchie Rajah, and the prince was so surprised to see a poor man carrying such costly bangles that he stopped and began to question him. "Those are very handsome jewels," said he.

"I have never seen finer. Even I myself have none like them. Tell me, how did you come by them?"

"They are not mine," answered the bangle-seller; "they belong to an old seven-headed cobra who lives down by the river. He gave them to me to make into bangles for a young prince named Muchie Lai, who lives with him."

The Rajah was very much surprised at what the bangle-seller told him. "This is a strange story," said he. "I will go with you, for I should like to see this young prince who lives in a cobra's hole."

So Muchie Rajah went down to the river bank with the bangle-seller. Muchie Lai was there playing close to the cobra's hole with the young cobras. When he saw the bangle-seller he ran to meet him, calling to him to know whether he had brought the bangles; and the young prince was so exactly like his mother, the beautiful Balna, that the Rajah was filled with joy and sorrow.

"Tell me, child," he cried, "who are you, and who was your mother?"

"I am Muchie Lai," answered the boy, "and my mother is the Ranee Balna, and we live here by the river in the hole of an old seven-headed cobra."

Then Muchie Rajah knelt down by the cobra's hole and called, "Oh, my dear wife, if it is you, and you are still alive, answer me!"

Balna heard his voice down in the cobra's hole, and came running out and threw herself into his arms.

"Oh, I have waited for you so long," she cried, "but you have come at last, and now I can go back with you to the palace."

So they were very happy. Only the cobra was sad to have them go, and the cobra's children were grieved to lose their little playmate. But he promised them to come back sometimes and play with them there by the river.

Then the Rajah and the Ranee and Muchie Lai all went back to the palace together, and there was great rejoicing.

But when the fakir's wife and her daughter heard that Balna was still alive, and that her husband had found her, they were so frightened that they ran away and hid themselves in the deep forest, and no one has ever heard of them again from that day to this.

Source: "The Fish Prince," Katharine Pyle. *Wonder Tales from Many Lands.* (London: George G. Harrap, Ltd., 1910), pp. 146–159.

Benito, the Faithful Servant

The essential characteristics of the following Filipino hero tale suggest a European origin, but specific environmental features show the story's adaptation to a traditional Philippine environment. The appeal of this sort of narrative to the Filipino community in the United States is found in the theme of an industrious man of humble origin finding success in spite of apparently overwhelming obstacles.

On a time there lived in a village a poor man and his wife, who had a son named Benito. The one ambition of the lad from his earliest youth was that he might be a help to the family in their struggle for a living.

But the years went by, and he saw no opportunity until one day, as they sat at dinner, his father fell to talking about the young King who lived at a distance from the village, in a beautiful palace kept by a retinue of servants. The boy was glad to hear this, and asked his parents to let him become one of the servants of this great ruler. The mother protested, fearing that her son could not please his Royal Majesty; but the boy was so eager to try his fortune that at last he was permitted to do so.

The next day his mother prepared food for him to eat on the journey, and he started for the palace. The journey was tiresome, and when he reached the palace he had difficulty in obtaining an audience with the King. But when he succeeded and made known his wish, the monarch detected a charming personality hidden within the ragged clothes, and, believing the lad would make a willing servant, he accepted him.

The servants of his Majesty had many duties. Theirs was not a life of ease, but of hard work. The very next day the King called Benito, and said, "I want you to bring me a certain beautiful princess who lives in a land across the sea; and if you fail to do it, you will be punished."

Benito did not know how he was to do it; but he asked no questions, and unhesitatingly answered, "I will, my lord."

That same day he provided himself with everything he needed for the journey and set off. He traveled a long distance until he came to the heart of a thick forest, where he saw a large bird which said to him, "Oh, my friend! Please take away these strings that are wrapped all about me. If you will, I will help you whenever you call upon me."

Benito released the bird and asked it its name. It replied, "Sparrow-hawk," and flew away.

Benito continued his journey until he came to the seashore. There he could see no way of getting across, and, remembering what the King had said if he failed, he stood looking out over the sea, feeling very sad.

The huge King of the Fishes saw him, and swam toward him. "Why are you so sad?" asked the Fish.

"I wish to cross the sea to find the beautiful Princess," replied the youth.

"Get on my back and I will take you across," said the King of the Fishes.

Benito rode on the back of the Fish and crossed the sea. As soon as he reached the other side, a fairy in the form of a woman appeared to him, and became a great aid to him in his adventure. She knew exactly what he wanted; so she told him that the Princess was shut up in a castle guarded by giants, and that he would have to fight the giants before he could reach her. For this purpose she gave him a magic sword, which would kill on the instant anything it touched. Benito now felt sure he could take the Princess from her cruel guardsmen. He went to the castle, and there he saw many giants round about it. When the giants saw him coming, they went out to meet him, thinking to take him captive. They were so sure that they could easily do it, that they went forth unarmed. As they came near, he touched the foremost ones with his sword, and one after another they fell down dead. The other giants, seeing so many of their number slain, became terrified, and fled, leaving the castle unguarded.

The young man went to the Princess and told her that his master had sent him to bring her to his palace. The young Princess was only too glad to leave the land of the giants, where she had been held captive. So the two set out together for the King's palace.

When they came to the sea they rode across it on the back of the same fish that had carried Benito. They went through the forest, and at last came to the palace. Here they were received with the greatest rejoicings.

After a short time the King asked the Princess to become his wife. "I will, O King!" she replied, "if you will get the ring I lost in the sea as I was crossing it."

The monarch called Benito, and ordered him to find the ring which had been lost on their journey from the land of the giants.

Obedient to his master, Benito started, and travelled on and on till he came to the shore of the sea. There he stood, gazing sadly out over the waters, not knowing how he was to search for what lay at the bottom of the deep ocean.

Again the King of the Fishes came to him, asking the cause of his sadness. Benito replied, "The Princess lost her ring while we were crossing the sea, and I have been sent to find it."

The King-Fish summoned all the fishes to come to him. When they had assembled, he noticed that one was missing. He commanded the others to search for this one, and bring it to him. They found it under a stone, and it said, "I am so full! I have eaten so much that I cannot swim." So the larger ones took it by the tail and dragged it to their King.

"Why did you not come when summoned?" asked the King-Fish. "I was so full I could not swim," replied the Fish.

The King-Fish, suspecting that it had swallowed the ring, ordered it to be cut in two. The others cut it open, and, behold, there was the lost ornament. Benito thanked the King of the Fishes, took the ring, and brought it to the monarch.

When the great ruler got the ring, he said to the Princess, "Now that I have your ring, will you become my wife?"

"I will be your wife," replied the Princess, "if you will find the earring I lost in the forest as I was journeying with Benito."

Instantly Benito was called, and was ordered to find the lost jewel. He was very weary from his former journey; but, mindful of his duty, he started for the forest, reaching it before the day was over. He searched for the earring faithfully, following the road which he and the Princess had taken; but all in vain. He was much discouraged, and sat down under a tree to rest. To his surprise a mouse of monstrous size appeared before him. It was the King of the Mice.

"Why are you so sad?" asked the Mouse.

"I am searching for an earring which the Princess lost as we passed through the forest, but am unable to find it."

"I will find it for you," said the King-Mouse.

Benito's face brightened at hearing this. The King-Mouse called all his followers, and all but one little mouse responded. Then the King of the Mice ordered some of his subjects to find the absent one. They found him in a small hole among the bamboo-trees. He said he could not go because he was so satisfied (sated). So the others pulled him along to their master; and he, finding that there was something hard within the little mouse, ordered him to be cut open. It was done; and there was the very earring for which the tired servant was looking. Benito took it, thanked the King of the Mice, and brought the earring to his own King.

When the monarch received it, he immediately restored it to its owner and asked, "Will you now become my wife?"

"Oh, dear King!" responded the Princess, "I have only one more thing to ask of you; and if you will grant it, I will be your wife forever."

The King, pleased with his former successes, said, "Tell me what it is, and it shall be granted."

"If you will get some water from heaven," said the Princess, "and some water from the nether-world, I will become your wife. That is my last wish."

The King called Benito, and commanded him to get water from these two places. "I will, my King," said Benito; and he took some provisions and started. He came to the forest; but there he became confused, for he did not know in which direction to go to reach either of the places. Suddenly he recalled the promise of the bird he had helped the first time he entered the wood.

He called the bird, and it soon appeared. He told it what he wanted, and it said, "I will get it for you."

He made two cups of bamboo, and tied one to each of the bird's legs. They were very light, and did not hinder the bearer at all. Away the bird flew, going very fast. Before the day was ended, it came back with each cup full of water, and told Benito that the one tied to its right leg contained water from heaven, and the one tied to its left leg contained water from the nether-world.

Benito untied the cups, taking great care of them. He was about to leave, when the bird asked him to tarry long enough to bury it, as the places to which it had been were so far away that it was weary unto death.

Benito did not like to bury the bird, but he soon saw that it really was dying, so he waited; and when it was dead, he buried it, feeling very sorry over the loss of so helpful a friend. He went back to the palace and delivered the two kinds of water to his master. The Princess then asked the King to cut her in two and pour the water from heaven upon her. The King was not willing to do it, so she did it herself, asking the King to pour the water. This he did, and, the Princess turned into the most beautiful woman that ever the sun shone on.

Then the King was desirous of becoming handsome; so he asked the Princess to pour the other cup of water over him after he cut himself. He cut himself, and she poured over his body the water from the nether-world; but from him there arose a spirit more ugly and ill-favored than imagination could picture. Fortunately, it soon vanished from sight.

The Princess then turned to Benito, and said, "You have been faithful in your duties to your master, kind to me in restoring the jewels I lost, and brave in delivering me from the cruel giants. You are the man I choose for my husband."

Benito could not refuse so lovely a lady. They were married amid great festivities, and became the king and queen of that broad and fertile land.

Benito gave his parents one of the finest portions of his kingdom, and furnished them with everything they could desire. From that time on they were all very happy,—so happy that the story of their bliss has come down through the centuries to us.

Source: "Benito, The Faithful Servant," Clara Kern Bayliss. "Philippine Folk-Tales," *Journal of American Folklore* 21 (1908): 46–53, pp. 50–53.

The Story of Four Friends

Americans of Indian descent note that tales of this sort have value as entertainment, as cultural artifacts that give a feeling of connectedness to a prized heritage, and as guides for proper social behavior. In this case, four friends from very different backgrounds join together to win a princess. The emphasis in the tale is on the value of cooperation by requiring each friend to provide his special talents in the service of the one among them who would finally be the successful suitor.

Once upon a time there lived four friends. One was the son of a king, another of a goldsmith, the third of a pandit [a scholar, a "pundit"], and the fourth of a carpenter. The four friends used to wrestle together, and all were very brave and powerful.

One day as they were wrestling, a giant came and made an enclosure of four walls around them, and challenged the four friends to try their strength on it by breaking it down. All tried in vain, but none succeeded, except the king's son, who broke the enclosure. On this the giant said: "You are the strongest of all, so go to Loha Garh or Iron Fort. There live a giant and a beautiful princess worthy of you. Go there and kill the giant; so you will be known as the strongest man and get the most beautiful princess that ever breathed."

The king's son was fired by the idea of getting her, and with the permission of his father at once started for the place. In the way he met his three friends, who accompanied him. They traveled on and on till they came to a lonely place where there was a well. Finding the place very pleasant and romantic they halted there.

Three went out to hunt, and the fourth, the goldsmith's son, began to prepare food. As he was cooking, a giant came out of the well and said: "Give me something out of this food."

The goldsmith's son replied, "I have not yet given to any *pir* [religious leader] or *faqir* ["fakir," mystic or magician], how can I give thee? Sit down; when my friends will come, thou shalt also get something."

On this the giant caught him by the wrist and threw him aside and took away all the food. When the friends came they did not find any food ready. On learning the cause, another friend, the carpenter's son, volunteered to cook and fight the giant while the three went out to hunt. He met the same adventure. So did the third. At last the king's son volunteered to cook. The giant came out as usual and asked for food.

The king's son said: "The bread has not been given as yet, to pir or faqir, how dare you ask for it? Wait and you will get."

On this the giant caught hold of the wrist of the king's son, and the latter caught hold of the other's hand, and there was a regular fight. At last the king's son threw him down into the well and followed him into it and had a long fight there. When the giant, whose name was Tasma Shah, was perfectly subdued, he agreed to purchase peace by accompanying the prince in his journey and marrying his daughter to him. But the prince, who was in search of the lady of Loha Garh, declined the latter offer, but negotiated the match for his friend, the goldsmith's son.

So as soon as the marriage was solemnized, the three friends leaving the married couple behind started forward on their journey. Though they had lost one of their playmates, yet their number was not lessened, for the giant, Tasma Shah, true to his promise, accompanied them and proved of great service to them by his courage, devotion and fidelity to the prince. The three friends and the giant proceeded on their journey.

They reached a city which was desolate, and where all the shops were closed. But in the midst of a large square there was only one living creature; she was a very beautiful girl with a basket full of flowers.

On seeing them she began to weep and said, "Go away from this place. Do not stop here; for, this city is infested by a terrible giant who will soon come and devour you all."

The giant Tasma Shah, who by the way, had assumed the shape of a man, for giants can put on any shape they like, said, "Never mind! We will stop here." Then they all stopped there for the night.

The three friends, being tired, soon fell asleep, and Tasma Shah kept watch. As he was watching, he saw a very tall giant, whose head touched the sky, coming towards him; seeing him Tasma Shah rolled himself on the ground and resumed his original shape of a giant which was so long kept disguised under that of a man. He enlarged his height, and expanded his form to the utmost, but could not reach higher than the shoulders of the giant of the city. Both then began to fight, and there was a great fight between them, so that the walls of the city shook and trembled. At last Tasma Shah killed the other giant.

By this time it was dawn. The carcass of the dead giant fell with a loud crash on the city and stretched for many a mile.

When the king of the city learned the news of the giant's death from the women, he was very much astonished and pleased. For this giant was a very cruel one, and used to eat ten citizens every day, and had almost eaten away the whole city. The king searched out the four persons, and offered the hand of his daughter to Tasma Shah. But the latter generously recommended his friend, the pandit's son, instead.

So the second friend was married, and the two remaining friends and the giant, Tasma Shah, proceeded on their journey. They reached another city which was equally silent and desolate. They saw many pots full of milk and a very beautiful boy standing near them. On the friends enquiring why he was standing there alone, and why the shops were all closed, the boy said: "There comes a lion here, and he takes away daily a man and ten pots of milk. This day it is my lot to be devoured by the lion, and those pots, which you see, are for him. Do not stop here, but please go away." The three travelers gave hope to the boy, and promised to help him.

So the king's son and the carpenter's son both slept, while Tasma Shah kept watch. At last, when it was midnight, the lion came with a loud roar. But as soon as Tasma Shah saw the lion, he ran towards him and killed him.

When in the morning the vizier of the city passed on that side on his inspecting tour, he saw the dead lion and the four persons including the boy. The vizier asked them: "Who has killed the lion?" On learning the fact he took them before the Raja, who, in reward for this good service, gave in marriage his daughter to the carpenter's son.

Then the king's son and the giant, Tasma Shah, proceeded on their journey towards Loha Garh, thus leaving one by one all their friends behind. At last they reached their destination. In that fort they saw a beautiful lady sitting on a tower. The giant took the prince on his back, and jumped into the fort and placed him before the beautiful lady. She strongly warned the prince to leave the fort, telling him that it was haunted by a giant. But the prince assured her that the horrible giant was already killed, and, so in fact it was, for in the meantime Tasma Shah had killed the giant of the fort.

So the prince began to live with the lady. The prince lived in the tower, and Tasma Shah lived downstairs. The latter vowed never to go upstairs, which he held sacred, and received his food from the king's son who brought it down daily for him. The lady of the fort one day went out to bathe in an adjacent stream.

She unfortunately lost her shoe in the stream. The shoe floating away touched the coast of a city where a Raja's son was bathing. The Raja's son took up the shoe, and finding it was a lady's shoe, preserved it carefully and fell in love with its unknown wearer. So he went home and sat in a corner moodily. When the king came and asked his son the reason, the prince said: "I will not live, if I do not get the person whose shoe this is, for my wife."

The king hearing this, and finding that advice will be no remedy for the incurable malady of his son, promised to give him that lady in marriage. So the king called the witches of the place and asked them to bring the lady whose shoe it was.

One of the witches who knew the spell to control streams, rivers and waters, undertook the task. So she chanted some charms, and dived into the stream and reached the fort of Loha Garh. She went near the tower and began to weep. The lady of the tower saw her, and calling her up hastily, was taken in by her specious tale of misery, and kept her as her servant.

When the witch had remained there for some time, one day she advised her mistress to ask the prince the secret of his life and death. The lady of the fort, not fearing any mischief, asked the prince, and was told by him that his life lay in the brightness of his sword. As long as the sword remained bright and untarnished, he would be alive, but no sooner was it rusty than he would die.

When the foolish princess told this secret to the witch, the latter rejoiced very much in her heart. The evil woman was always on the look out for an opportunity to execute her wicked design. So one night when all had gone to sleep, the witch stole into the prince's room, took the charmed sword and put it into a burning furnace where it soon lost its brightness, and at that very moment the young prince lost his life. As soon as he was dead, the witch took up the sleeping princess and conveyed her under the stream to the Raja's son. The Raja and his son were very much pleased to get hold of the beautiful lady. But when the princess awoke, and found that she had been brought to this pass, she mustered all her courage, and her good sense soon devised a means of escape. She asked the Raja and his son to wait for a year, after which period she would marry the Raja's son. The Raja agreed to this, but kept the princess in close confinement in a strong fort.

Here Tasma Shah began to starve, for the prince being dead no one brought food for him. When he had passed a week without food he resolved to find out what was the matter. So once for all, breaking through his self-imposed vow, he went upstairs and with one glance took in the whole situation. He at once ran to the furnace, took out the sword and searched carefully whether any portion of it was bright or not. After a good search he found the tip of the sword still retaining its brightness, as it had been thrust into the earth and had not been burned. So Tasma Shah began to rub the sword, and after great efforts restored its brightness to the weapon and life to its prince. Then the two went out in search of the lost princess. They first got all the other friends together.

After great search the friends went to the city where the princess was kept a prisoner. They reached the city a few days before the expiration of the year of grace. Great preparations were being made for the coming marriage.

They consulted together about the means of having a talk with the princess and giving news of their arrival. At last the pandit's son in the guise of an astrologer entered the fort, and under pretence of telling her fortune told the princess that the prince was in the city, and had devised some means for her release and told her what it was. A day before the marriage the princess said to the Raja that it was the custom of her family to float round the city in a golden aerial car with the bridegroom and the matchmaker. The Raja, seeing that there could be no harm in indulging her in this whim, consented that she should have her wish, and sent his men to fetch such a car.

In the meanwhile the giant, Tasma Shah, with the help of the goldsmith's son and the carpenter's son, had constructed such a car and brought it for sale to the Raja. The Raja bought the wonderful car and sat on it with the princess, his son, and the witch and began to move in the air round the city.

When the princess told them to stop at a certain place and the car was stopped, the four friends, headed by Tasma Shah, jumped into the car and moving its hidden spring at once rose very high into the air. They then bound down the treacherous witch, the Raja and his son, and drowned them in the river for their wickedness and returned gloriously to their city.

Source: "The Four Friends," Shaikh Chilli. *Folk-Tales of Hindustan, 2nd edition.* (Calcutta: Abinash Chandra Shakar, 1913), pp. 38–44.

The Grass-Cutting Sword

In spite of the approximate dates and the names of historical individuals provided in the following narrative, the tale walks a fine line between myth and legend. At least as important as the exploits of Yamato-dake no Mikoto is the confirmation of the sacred status of the "Grass-Cutting Sword," a weapon that received its name in recognition of its powers to thwart the assassination attempt on the protagonist in Suruga Province. The tale has been considered essential to the education of Japanese Americans with a desire to maintain a sense of traditional heritage.

About the year 110 B.C. there lived a brave prince known in Japanese history as Yamato-dake no Mikoto. He was a great warrior, as was his son, who is said to have been a husband to the Empress Jingo—I presume a second one, for it could not have been the Emperor who was assassinated before the Empress's conquest of Korea. However, that does not very much matter to my story, which is merely the legend attached to the miraculous sword known as the Kusanagi no Tsurugi (the grass-cutting sword), which is held as one of the three sacred treasures, and is handed down from father to son in the Imperial Family. The sword is kept at the Atsuta Shrine, in Owari Province.

At the date given by my interpreter, 110 B.C. (I should add "or thereabouts," allowing large margins), Yamato-dake no Mikoto had been successful at all events in suppressing the revolutionists known as the Kumaso in Kyushu. Being a man of energy, and possessing a strong force of trained men, he resolved that he would suppress the revolutionists up on the northeastern coasts.

Before starting, Yamato-dake no Mikoto thought he should go to Ise to worship in the temples, to pray for divine aid, and to call on an aunt who lived near. Yamato-dake spent five or six days with his aunt, Princess Yamato Hime, to whom he announced his intention of subduing the rebels. She presented him with her greatest treasure—the miraculous sword—and also with a tinder-and-flint-box.

Before parting with her nephew Yamato Hime no Mikoto said: "This sword is the most precious thing which I could give you, and will guard you safely through all dangers. Value it accordingly, for it will be one of the sacred treasures.''

(Legend says that in the age of the gods Susanoo-no Mikoto once found an old man and a woman weeping bitterly because a mammoth eight-headed snake had devoured seven of their daughters, and there remained only one more, whom, they felt sure, the eighth serpent's head would take. Susanoo-no Mikoto asked if they would give him the daughter if he killed the snake to which they gladly assented. Susanoo filled eight buckets with sake-wine, and put them where the serpent was likely to come, and, hiding himself in the vicinity, awaited events. The monster came, and the eight heads drank the eight buckets full of sake, and became, naturally, dead-drunk. Susanoo then dashed in and cut the beast to bits. In the tail he found a sword—the celebrated and miraculous sword Kusanagi no Tsurugi, the grass-cutting sword of our story.)

After bidding farewell to Yamato Hime no Mikoto, the Prince took his departure, setting out for the province of Suruga, on the eastern coast, to find what he could hear, it being in a turbulent state; and it was there that he ran into his first danger, and that his enemies laid a trap for him, through their knowledge that he was fond of hunting.

There were some immense rush plains in Suruga Province where now stands the village of Yaitsu Mura ("Yaita" means "burning fields"). It was resolved by the rebels that one of them should go and invite Yamato-dake to come out and hunt, while they were to scatter and hide themselves in the long grass, until the guide should lead him into their midst, when they would jump up and kill him. Accordingly, they sent to Yamato-dake a plausible and clever man, who told him that there were many deer on the grass plains. Would he come and hunt them? The man volunteered to act as guide. The invitation was tempting; and, as he had found the country less rebellious than he had expected, the Prince accepted.

When the morning arrived the Prince, in addition to carrying his hunting-bow, carried the sword given him by his aunt, the Princess Yamato. The day was windy, and it was thought by the rebels that as the rushes were so dry it would be more sure, and less dangerous to themselves, to fire the grass, for it was certain that the guide would make the Prince hunt upwind, and if they fired the grass properly the flames would rush with lightning speed towards him and be absolutely safe for themselves.

Yamato-dake did just as they had expected. He came quietly on, suspecting nothing. Suddenly the rushes took fire in front and at the sides of him. The Prince realized that he had been betrayed. The treacherous guide had disappeared. The Prince stood in danger of suffocation and death. The smoke, dense and choking, rushed along with rapidity and great roaring. Yamato-dake tried to run for the only gap, but was too late. Then he began cutting the grass with his sword, to prevent the fire from reaching him. He found that whichever direction he cut in with his sword, the wind changed to that direction. If to the north he cut, the wind changed to the south and prevented the fire from advancing farther; if to the south, the wind changed to the north; and so on. Taking advantage of this, Yamato-dake retaliated upon his enemies. He got fire from his aunt's tinder-box, and where there was no fire in the rushes he lit them, cutting through the grass at the same time in the direction in which he wished the fire to go. Rushing thus from point to point, he was successful in the endeavour to turn the tables on his enemies, and destroyed them all. It is important to note that there is in existence a sword, said to be this sword, in the Atsuta Shrine, Owari Province; a great festival in honour of it is held on June 21 every year.

From that place Yamato-dake no Mikoto went on to Sagami Province. Finding things quiet there, he took a ship to cross to Kazusa Province, accompanied by a lady he deeply loved, who was given the title of Hime (Princess) because of Yamato-dake's rank. Her name was Tachibana. They had not got more than ten miles from shore when a terrible storm arose. The ship threatened to go down.

"This," said Tachibana Hime, "is the doing of one of the sea-goddesses who thirst for men's lives. I will give her mine, my lord; perhaps that may appease her until you have safely crossed the wicked sea."

Without further warning, Tachibana Hime cast herself into the sea; the waves closed over her head, to the consternation and grief of all, and to the breaking of Yamato-dake's heart. As Tachibana Hime had expected, the sea-goddess was appeased. The wind went down, the water calmed, and the ship reached Kazusa Province in safety. Yamato-dake went as far as Yezo, putting down small rebellions on the way.

Several years afterwards, accompanied by many of his old officers, he found himself back on the side of a hill in Sagami Province overlooking the place where poor Tachibana Hime had given up her life for him by throwing herself into the sea. The Prince gazed sadly at the sea, and thrice exclaimed, with tears flowing down his cheeks,—brave though he was—"Azuma waya!" (Alas, my dearest wife!); and Eastern Japan, about the middle, has since then been called "Azuma."

Source: "A Miraculous Sword," Richard Gordon Smith. *Ancient Tales and Folklore of Japan.* (London: A. and C. Black, 1908), pp. 56–60.

Han Hsin

The existence of Chinese General Han Hsin is historically docu-mented. In fact, the earliest written account (200 B.C.E.) of kite flying dates to Han Hsin's use of a kite for military surveillance. On the other hand, aspects of his story such as his having been fed on tiger's milk, his use of superior wit to compensate for an unimposing physical stat-ure, and his precociousness fall neatly into the archetype of the legen-dary folk hero. As such he has been remembered in Chinese legendary history and among Americans of Chinese descent.

The youth of Western lands know very little of the great land of China, with its long history reaching far back into the dim past. How little is known of the fierce, stupendous struggles in the long ago, when China was not one country but was composed of many small kingdoms whose people were constantly fighting with each other for supremacy.

It was in those early days that were born China's heroes who have been remembered ever since in song and story. To the Chinese but little stage setting is necessary for their national heroes. In their theatrical plays their imaginations fill in, with the help of mere suggestions, all that is needed to make their surroundings very real to them.

One of China's greatest heroes was Han Hsin. He lived in the kingdom of Chin, very many centuries ago. When he was a small boy he showed remark-able wisdom, and, although he was very small of stature, his teachers predicted a great future for him.

One day, when Han was only six years old, he and another little boy were playing ball, when the ball came down into the deep hole of the millstones. They could not get it out at first and the other lad wanted to call for help.

Little Han Hsin said, "No, I will think of a plan." Finding a long stick, he began filling the hole with earth. As he poured the earth into the hole, he kept stirring the ball around, thereby keeping it on top of the earth until he could reach it with his hand.

Another time he saw a woman, in rage, jump into a large earthen water-barrel. He was not strong enough to draw her out, and no one was near, so he found a stone and beat with all his strength on the barrel until he made a hole in it near the bottom, and the water running out, the life of the woman was saved. Many such stories, and more wonderful ones, were told of him, and his fame spread all over the kingdom.

In those days every prince had a wise man, or a group of wise men, about him to give him advice regarding the affairs of his kingdom. Han Hsin was presented to his Prince by his teachers as worthy of holding such a position, but when the Prince and his officers saw how small he was, they laughed and said, " We do not want a child," and would not accept his services.

Han Hsin then went and presented himself at the court of the Prince of Chin Chou. Now, this Prince, Chin Pa, was noted for his strength. It was said of him that, if he tried, he could breathe the roof off the house; also that he could lift himself up by the hair. When he was small he was fed on the milk of the tiger. Thus his strength was not the strength of man.

When Han Hsin was presented to this Prince by his teachers as a wise man and one who could help him make his country strong, he laughed and said, "What can such a boy do? If I hold out my head and tell him to cut it off he has not the strength to do it, even though I stand still and do not resist him. How can there be wisdom in such a small boy? How can such as he help me? He cannot fight for me or wait on me. Take away the child, I do not want him."

The teachers urged the Prince to give the young man a trial and at last he said, "Here is my spear let him hold it up straight for half a day. If he is strong enough for that, he may find something to do in my service." Alas! Han Hsin could not even for half an hour hold up the great iron spear, and he was driven with laughter and derision from the court.

When the teachers remonstrated with the Prince he said, "I want no such weakling in my kingdom."

"But you have made an enemy of him," they urged, "and if you do not use him, you should kill him. Although you, our Prince, will not believe us, we know if you let him go he will, in the end, be used by some other kingdom to destroy yours."

At this Chin Pa laughed loud and long, but seeing the anxious and serious faces of the teachers he said, "I will take some soldiers and go after him, and if you wish I will kill him."

Now when Han Hsin, in bitterness of heart, was driven from the court he took the road leading to the mountains, and was part way up when, chancing to look back, he saw the mounted band coming. They did not see him, but he knew that they were in search of him. He knew that he could not escape, so he stretched himself out on the side of the hill with his feet toward the top and his head toward the bottom of the hill, and pretended that he was asleep.

When Chin Pa came up and saw him there he smiled to himself and called to his men to remount, and away they went back to the castle, laughing and making merry over the thought that any one who would sleep in such a position, could rend the kingdom away from their great Prince.

When the teachers heard of the outcome of the pursuit of Han Hsin they were troubled and said, "It is craft and not stupidity go back again, overtake him and kill him." To please them and for the sport of it, the Prince started out again.

By this time Han Hsin had crossed the mountains and was walking on the plain. Again he saw them coming, and looking about he discovered a very ill-smelling hole, and bending over it he exclaimed, as his pursuers came up, "Ah, how sweet, how fragrant!"

This time the Prince declared that Han Hsin was entirely foolish, and he would not kill a fool, for a man who did not know the difference between the sweetly fragrant and the offensive was not one a Prince need fear.

Thus Han Hsin was left to himself, and returned to his own country and village. His own Prince, Han Kao Lin, again refused him. At that time this Prince was at war with Chin Pa and was very hard pressed by the latter, and anxious to surround himself with wise men. He could not see, however, how there could be wisdom in such a small man as Han Hsin. But, at last, after much persuasion, he gave a reluctant permission for him to be made leader of the army which was about to set out to attack Chin Pa.

Old pictures show Han Hsin seated on a throne and worshipped by the military men and soldiers under him. They believed that he was to lead them to victory and save their country. It is said that he knew every soldier, and could tell at a glance how many there were in a company passing before him and who were absent from the ranks. He was one of the greatest military leaders, if not the greatest, in Chinese history.

One time, when engaged in war with the Kingdom of Chao, he drove the enemy to the bank of a river, but they got over in their own boats and destroyed them on the other side. Feeling secure in the thought that the army under Han Hsin could not cross that night, they made a camp and had a feast. But Han Hsin was not an ordinary man and he commanded every man to get a board of some kind and in the darkness to swim across quietly. This they did, and fell upon the merry camp and won a great victory.

Another time Han Hsin insisted on camping on the shore of the great river. His officers and men protested, and said that he was not leaving any path for retreat in case of defeat, as they had no ships or bridges and few could swim so far. All the comfort they could get was his reply, "When defeat comes we will discuss the question." The enemy were seen coming upon them from the front, and then Han Hsin called to his men to fight for their lives, for death was certainly behind them in the river, but, if they fought bravely, they could defeat the enemy in front. This they did with great slaughter.

At another time, when fighting with the great Chin Pa, of the Kingdom of Chin, the latter shut up all but one of the roads over the mountains and awaited Han Hsin in ambuscade in a very narrow place, the only one where it seemed possible for him to get over the mountains. He did not even then know the military master that he had to deal with in Han Hsin, as it was still early in the war. Han Hsin sent out his spies, disguised as countrymen, and learned the condition of things. So, calling up his men to make a lot of bags, even turning their clothes into bags, his army set out.

On reaching the steepest place in ascending the mountains, he commanded the army to halt and fill the bags with earth. This place was not guarded, as it was supposed to be impossible of ascent. During the night, however, Han Hsin ordered an advance, and, using the bags to make a series of steps, his army went quickly up and over to the other side, to the rear of Chin Pa's army. Here Han Hsin attacked the enemy in force and easily put them to flight. Later they recovered themselves and in many battles afterward between these two great generals neither could obtain any great advantage.

Now Han Hsin had a friend and helper in Chang Lang, a literary man who was wise and safe to trust, and who often helped him in his plans. They talked over the situation, and Chang Lang said that the strength of Chin Pa was in a company of three thousand soldiers who were all related to each other, and whose officers were also of the same clan. In some way that company must be disbanded or Han Hsin never would win the final victory. Many plans were formed, but the soldiers of the clan seemed to possess charmed lives.

At last Chang Lang came one night to the tent of Han Hsin and said, "I have found a way, and, as there is a fine wind and it is on the eve of a battle, I will try my new scheme." He then produced a large kite, the first ever made, and disclosed his plan. All these years Han Hsin had remembered how Chin Pa had laughed at his small stature, but he was that night to show him that, though small, he was formidable as an enemy.

Some of his officers were called in and fastened him by ropes to the kite and then let go. Gradually the kite ascended, and, in the twilight, appeared high over the camp of the three thousand soldiers. They were filled with terror, for never before had such a thing been seen or heard of. It was dark enough to prevent them from seeing Han Hsin at the height and distance he was from them. The kite came to rest for a few moments, and they heard a voice say, "You all have old and young in your homes. Why do you not go home to them? If you stay on, you will some day all be killed; then who will worship at the grave of your fathers and hand down the name?"

The men said, "It is a voice of a god, a warning, let us depart at once," and that night they left the camp.

The battle the next day was terrific, but in the end Han Hsin won a great victory. When urged to kill his old enemy he said, "No, let him go, for he will kill himself, and that will be better." So, Chin Pa was set at liberty and started with his army to return south. The battle had been near a river and Han Hsin knew that Chin Pa must cross it on his retreat. So, before the battle was fought, Han Hsin had written, in honey, on a big stone slab near the ford, these four words, "Heaven Destroy Hsiang Yi." The last two words were Chin Pa's name. A swarm of ants scenting the honey crawled up to eat it, and thus outlined the characters very distinctly.

When Chin Pa came over the river and saw the stone with the four large characters he said, "Woe is me, even the worms and ants know that Heaven has deserted me. I will kill myself." And then and there, almost in sight of his enemy, the man he had regarded with contempt, he killed himself.

Thus ended a strife of nearly twenty years between two kingdoms, and Han Hsin came to be the Prince of his kingdom. Often during the time of kite-flying in China, away in the heavens one sees a kite in the shape of an old-time warrior, and few of the many beautiful and fancy kites to be seen have such an interesting story. The kite has come to be, in Western lands, merely an amusement, but in China, where it was probably invented, it ever carries with the sport the message, "Strength of mind is greater than strength of body."

Source: "Han Hsin," Norman Hinsdale Pitman. *A Chinese Wonder Book.* (New York: E.P. Dutton & Company, 1919), pp. 60–70.

The Ogre of Rashomon

The following tale was one of the fictional narratives of the feudal period that was transported by Japanese immigrants to the United States prior to the Second World War. The most elaborate versions of the story were preserved by adults who learned the story while still residing in Japan. "The Ogre of Rashomon," often under alternate titles (for example, "Oyeyama"), was passed along to subsequent Japanese American generations.

Long, long ago in Kyoto, the people of the city were terrified by accounts of a dreadful ogre, who, it was said, haunted the Gate of Rashomon at twilight and seized whoever passed by. The missing victims were never seen again, so it was whispered that the ogre was a horrible cannibal, who not only killed the unhappy victims but ate them also. Now everybody in the town and neighborhood was in great fear, and no one durst venture out after sunset near the Gate of Rashomon.

Now at this time there lived in Kyoto a general named Raiko, who had made himself famous for his brave deeds. Some time before this he made the country ring with his name, for he had attacked Oeyama, where a band of ogres lived with their chief, who instead of wine drank the blood of human beings. He had routed them all and cut off the head of the chief monster.

This brave warrior was always followed by a band of faithful knights. In this band there were five knights of great valor. One evening as the five knights sat at a feast quaffing saké in their rice bowls and eating all kinds of fish, raw, and stewed, and broiled, and toasting each other's healths and exploits, the first knight, Hojo, said to the others, "Have you all heard the rumor that every evening after sunset there comes an ogre to the Gate of Rashomon, and that he seizes all who pass by?"

The second knight, Watanabe, answered him, saying: "Do not talk such nonsense! All the ogres were killed by our chief Raiko at Oeyarna! It cannot be true, because even if any ogres did escape from that great killing they would not dare to show themselves in this city, for they know that our brave master would at once attack them if he knew that any of them were still alive!"

"Then do you disbelieve what I say, and think that I am telling you a falsehood?"

"No, I do not think that you are telling a lie," said Watanabe; "but you have heard some old woman's story which is not worth believing."

"Then the best plan is to prove what I say, by going there yourself and finding out yourself whether it is true or not," said Hojo.

Watanabe, the second knight, could not bear the thought that his companion should believe he was afraid, so he answered quickly: "Of course, I will go at once and find out for myself!"

So Watanabe at once got ready to go; he buckled on his long sword and put on a coat of armor, and tied on his large helmet. When he was ready to start he said to the others: "Give me something so that I can prove I have been there!"

Then one of the men got a roll of writing paper and his box of Indian ink and brushes, and the four comrades wrote their names on a piece of paper.

"I will take this," said Watanabe, "and put it on the Gate of Rashomon, so tomorrow morning will you all go and look at it? I may be able to catch an ogre or two by then!" and he mounted his horse and rode off gallantly.

It was a very dark night, and there was neither moon nor star to light Watanabe on his way. To make the darkness worse a storm came on, the rain fell heavily and the wind howled like wolves in the mountains. Any ordinary man would have trembled at the thought of going out of doors, but Watanabe was a brave warrior and dauntless, and his honor and word were at stake, so he sped on into the night, while his companions listened to the sound of his horse's hoofs dying away in the distance, then shut the sliding shutters close and gathered round the charcoal fire and wondered what would happen and whether their comrade would encounter one of those horrible oni.

At last Watanabe reached the Gate of Rashomon, but peer as he might through the darkness he could see no sign of an ogre. "It is just as I thought," said Watanabe to himself; "there are certainly no ogres here; it is only an old woman's story. I will stick this paper on the gate so that the others can see I have been here when they come tomorrow, and then I will take my way home and laugh at them all."

He fastened the piece of paper, signed by all his four companions, on the gate, and then turned his horse's head towards home. As he did so he became aware that some one was behind him, and at the same time a voice called out to him to wait. Then his helmet was seized from the back.

"Who are you?" said Watanabe fearlessly. He then put out his hand and groped around to find out who or what it was that held him by the helmet. As he did so he touched something that felt like an arm, it was covered with hair and as big round as the trunk of a tree! Watanabe knew at once that this was the arm of an ogre, so he drew his sword and cut at it fiercely.

There was a loud yell of pain, and then the ogre dashed in front of the warrior.

Watanabe's eyes grew large with wonder, for he saw that the ogre was taller than the great gate, his eyes were flashing like mirrors in the sunlight, and his huge mouth was wide open, and as the monster breathed, flames of fire shot out of his mouth.

The ogre thought to terrify his foe, but Watanabe never flinched. He attacked the ogre with all his strength, and thus they fought face to face for a long time. At last the ogre, finding that he could neither frighten nor beat Watanabe and that he might himself be beaten, took to flight. But Watanabe, determined not to let the monster escape, put spurs to his horse and gave chase. But though the knight rode very fast the ogre ran faster, and to his disappointment he found himself unable to overtake the monster, who was gradually lost to sight.

Watanabe returned to the gate where the fierce fight had taken place, and got down from his horse. As he did so he stumbled upon something lying on the ground.

Stooping to pick it up he found that it was one of the ogre's huge arms which he must have slashed off in the fight. His joy was great at having secured such a prize, for this was the best of all proofs of his adventure with the ogre. So he took it up carefully and carried it home as a trophy of his victory.

When he got back, he showed the arm to his comrades, who one and all called him the hero of their band and gave him a great feast. His wonderful deed was soon noised abroad in Kyoto, and people from far and near came to see the ogre's arm.

Watanabe now began to grow uneasy as to how he should keep the arm in safety, for he knew that the ogre to whom it belonged was still alive. He felt sure that one day or other, as soon as the ogre got over his scare, he would come to try to get his arm back again. Watanabe therefore had a box made of the strongest wood and banded with iron. In this he placed the arm, and then he sealed down the heavy lid, refusing to open it for any one. He kept the box in his own room and took charge of it himself, never allowing it out of his sight.

Now one night he heard some one knocking at the porch, asking for admittance. When the servant went to the door to see who it was, there was only an old woman, very respectable in appearance. On being asked who she was and what was her business, the old woman replied with a smile that she had been nurse to the master of the house when he was a little baby. If the lord of the house were at home she begged to be allowed to see him.

The servant left the old woman at the door and went to tell his master that his old nurse had come to see him. Watanabe thought it strange that she should come at that time of night, but at the thought of his old nurse, who had been like a foster-mother to him and whom he had not seen for a long time, a very tender feeling sprang up for her in his heart. He ordered the servant to show her in.

The old woman was ushered into the room, and after the customary bows and greetings were over, she said: "Master, the report of your brave fight with the ogre at the Gate of Rashomon is so widely known that even your poor old nurse has heard of it. Is it really true, what everyone says, that you cut off one of the ogre's arms? If you did, your deed is highly to be praised!"

"I was very disappointed," said Watanabe, "that I was not able to take the monster captive, which was what I wished to do, instead of only cutting off an arm!"

"I am very proud to think," answered the old woman, "that my master was so brave as to dare to cut off an ogre's arm. There is nothing that can be compared to your courage. Before I die it is the great wish of my life to see this arm," she added pleadingly.

"No," said Watanabe, "I am sorry, but I cannot grant your request."

"But why?" asked the old woman.

"Because," replied Watanabe, "ogres are very revengeful creatures, and if I open the box there is no telling but that the ogre may suddenly appear and carry off his arm. I have had a box made on purpose with a very strong lid, and in this box I keep the ogre's arm secure, and I never show it to anyone, whatever happens."

"Your precaution is very reasonable," said the old woman. "But I am your old nurse, so surely you will not refuse to show me the arm. I have only just heard of your brave act, and not being able to wait till the morning I came at once to ask you to show it to me."

Watanabe was very troubled at the old woman's pleading, but he still persisted in refusing. Then the old woman said, "Do you suspect me of being a spy sent by the ogre?"

"No, of course I do not suspect you of being the ogre's spy, for you are my old nurse," answered Watanabe.

"Then you cannot surely refuse to show me the arm any longer," entreated the old woman; "for it is the great wish of my heart to see for once in my life the arm of an ogre!"

Watanabe could not holdout in his refusal any longer, so he gave in at last, saying: "Then I will show you the ogre's arm, since you so earnestly wish to see it. Come, follow me!" and he led the way to his own room, the old woman following.

When they were both in the room Watanabe shut the door carefully, and then going towards a big box which stood in a corner of the room, he took off the heavy lid. He then called to the old woman to come near and look in, for he never took the arm out of the box.

"What is it like? Let me have a good look at it," said the old nurse, with a joyful face. She came nearer and nearer, as if she were afraid, till she stood right against the box. Suddenly she plunged her hand into the box and seized the arm, crying with a fearful voice which made the room shake: "Oh, joy! I have got my arm back again!"

And from an old woman she was suddenly transformed into the towering figure of the frightful ogre! Watanabe sprang back and was unable to move for a moment, so great was his astonishment, but recognizing the ogre who had attacked him at the Gate of Rashomon, he determined with his usual courage to put an end to him this time. He seized his sword, drew it out of its sheath in a flash, and tried to cut the ogre down.

So quick was Watanabe that the creature had a narrow escape. But the ogre sprang up to the ceiling, and bursting through the roof, disappeared in the mist and clouds. In this way the ogre escaped with his arm.

The knight gnashed his teeth with disappointment, but that was all he could do. He waited in patience for another opportunity to dispatch the ogre. But the latter was afraid of Watanabe's great strength and daring, and never troubled Kyoto again. So once more the people of the city were able to go out without fear even at night time, and the brave deeds of Watanabe have never been forgotten!

Source: "The Ogre of Rashomon," Yei Theodora Ozaki. *Japanese Fairy Tales.* (New York: Grosset and Dunlap, 1906), pp. 270–281.

Juan Pusong

Juan Pusong is a popular trickster figure in Filipino traditional tales. As is illustrated in the following cycle (group of tales involving the exploits of a particular stereotyped character), Juan fluctuates between the wily dimension of trickster and the trickster as overt "numskull" figure. His wiles are often tuned to malicious ends as in "Juan Gathers Guavas." The results of his foolishness are often unpredictable; for example, contrast "Juan Makes Gulay [Stew] of His Own Child" and "Juan Wins a Wager for the Governor." As "The Man in the Shroud" illustrates, however, no one else is able to accomplish intentionally what Juan achieves effortlessly.

Juan Gathers Guavas

The guavas were ripe, and Juan's father sent him to gather enough for the family and for the neighbors who came to visit them. Juan went to the guava bushes and ate all that he could hold. Then he began to look around for mischief.

He soon found a wasp nest and managed to get it into a tight basket. He gave it to his father as soon as he reached home, and then closed the door and fastened it. All the neighbors were inside waiting for the feast of guavas, and as soon as the basket was opened they began to fight to get out of the windows.

After a while Juan opened the door and when he saw his parents' swollen faces, he cried out, "What rich fine guavas those must have been! They have made you both so very fat."

Juan Makes *Gulay* [Stew] of His Own Child

After Juan was married about a year a baby was born, and he and his wife loved it very much. But Juan was always obedient to his wife, being a fool, and when she told him to make *gulay* or stew he inquired of her of what he should make it. She replied of *anac* [Tagalog, "child"], meaning *anac nang gabi* [Tagalog, "child of the night," the root of a local plant].

Then she went away for a while, and when she returned Juan had the *gulay* ready. She asked for the baby and was horrified to learn that Juan had made a stew of his own child, having taken her words literally.

Juan Wins a Wager for the Governor

Juan was well known for a brave man, though a fool, and the priest and the governor wished to try him on a wager. The governor told him that the priest was dead, and ordered him to watch the body in the church that night.

The priest lay down on the bier before the altar, and after Juan came the priest arose. Juan pushed him down again and ran out of the church and secured a club. Returning, he said to the priest, "You are dead; try to get up again and I will break you to pieces." So Juan proved himself to be a brave man, and the governor won his wager.

Juan Hides the Salt

Juan's father came into possession of a sack of salt, which used to be very precious and an expensive commodity. He wished it hidden in a secure place and so told Juan to hide it till they should need it.

Juan went out and after hunting for a long time hid it in a *carabao* [water buffalo] wallow, and of course when they went to fetch it again nothing was left but the sack.

The Man in the Shroud

Juan, being a joker, once thought to have a little fun at others' expense, so he robed himself in a shroud, placed a bier by the roadside, set candles around it, and lay down so that all who went by should see him and be frightened.

A band of robbers went by that way, and seeing the corpse, besought it to give them luck. As it happened, they were more than usually fortunate, and when they returned they began to make offerings to him to secure continuance of their good fortune. As the entire proceeds of their adventures were held in common, they soon began to quarrel over the offerings to be made. The captain became angry, and drew his sword with a threat to run the corpse through for causing so much dissension among his men.

This frightened the sham dead man to such a degree that he jumped up and ran away, and the robbers, who were even more frightened than he, ran the other way, leaving all their plunder.

Juan then returned and gathered all the money and valuables left behind by the robbers, and carried them home.

Now he had a friend who was very curious to know how he came into possession of so much wealth, and so Juan told him, only he said nothing about robbers, but told his friend, whose name was Pedro, that the things were the direct reward of God for his piety.

Pedro, being afraid of the woods, decided to lie just inside the church door; besides, that being a more sacred place, he felt sure that God would favor him even more than Juan. He arranged his bier with the candles around him, and lay down to await the shower of money that should reward his devotions. When the sacristan went to the church to ring the bell for vespers, he saw the body lying there, and not knowing of any corpse having been carried in, he was frightened and ran to tell the padre. The padre, when he had seen the body, said it was a miracle, and that it must be buried within the church, for the sanctification of the edifice.

But Pedro, now thoroughly frightened, jumped off the bier and ran away, and the priest and the sacristan ran the other way, so the poor man never received the reward for his piety, and the church was deprived of a new patron saint.

Source: "Tagalog Folk-Tales, I," Fletcher Gardner. *Journal of American Folklore* 20 (1907): pp. 104–116, 104–105.

The Farmer and the Badger

The "badger" of the following narrative is actually a "tanuki" (raccoon dog), an animal species native to Japan that figures in the nation's folklore. The folk tanuki is a comic trickster in most cases. There are even stories of tanuki assuming the shapes and roles of priests. The sinister quality of this tale's tanuki is a less common version of the character. When an older population of Japanese residents of California was questioned about this tale before the Second World War, they stated that it would be familiar to most of their community. A few years later during the internment ordeal of Americans of Japanese descent, rumors of the appearance of shape-shifting tanuki emerged in the internment camps.

Long, long ago, there lived an old farmer and his wife who had made their home in the mountains, far from any town. Their only neighbor was a bad and malicious badger. This badger used to come out every night and run across to the farmer's field and spoil the vegetables and the rice which the farmer spent his time in carefully cultivating. The badger at last grew so ruthless in his mischievous work, and did so much harm everywhere on the farm, that the good-natured farmer could not stand it any longer, and determined to put a stop to it. So he lay in wait day after day and night after night, with a big club, hoping to catch the badger, but all in vain. Then he laid traps for the wicked animal.

The farmer's trouble and patience was rewarded, for one fine day on going his rounds he found the badger caught in a hole he had dug for that purpose. The farmer was delighted at having caught his enemy, and carried him home securely bound with rope. When he reached the house the farmer said to his wife, "I have at last caught the bad badger. You must keep an eye on him while I am out at work and not let him escape, because I want to make him into soup tonight."

Saying this, he hung the badger up to the rafters of his storehouse and went out to his work in the fields. The badger was in great distress, for he did not at all like the idea of being made into soup that night, and he thought and thought for a long time, trying to hit upon some plan by which he might escape. It was hard to think clearly in his uncomfortable position, for he had been hung upside down. Very near him, at the entrance to the storehouse, looking out towards the green fields and the trees and the pleasant sunshine, stood the farmer's old wife pounding barley. She looked tired and old. Her face was seamed with many wrinkles, and was as brown as leather, and every now and then she stopped to wipe the perspiration which rolled down her face.

"Dear lady," said the wily badger, "you must be very weary doing such heavy work in your old age. Won't you let me do that for you? My arms are very strong, and I could relieve you for a little while!"

"Thank you for your kindness," said the old woman, "but I cannot let you do this work for me because I must not untie you, for you might escape if I did, and my husband would be very angry if he came home and found you gone."

Now, the badger is one of the most cunning of animals, and he said again in a very sad, gentle, voice, "You are very unkind. You might untie me, for I promise not to try to escape. If you are afraid of your husband, I will let you bind me again before his return when I have finished pounding the barley. I am so tired and sore tied up like this. If you would only let me down for a few minutes I would indeed be thankful!"

The old woman had a good and simple nature, and could not think badly of any one. Much less did she think that the badger was only deceiving her in order to get away. She felt sorry, too, for the animal as she turned to look at him. He looked in such a sad plight hanging downwards from the ceiling by his legs, which were all tied together so tightly that the rope and the knots were cutting into the skin. So in the kindness of her heart, and believing the creature's promise that he would not run away, she untied the cord and let him down.

The old woman then gave him the wooden pestle and told him to do the work for a short time while she rested. He took the pestle, but instead of doing the work as he was told, the badger at once sprang upon the old woman and knocked her down with the heavy piece of wood. He then killed her and cut her up and made soup of her, and waited for the return of the old farmer. The old man worked hard in his fields all day, and as he worked he thought with pleasure that no more now would his labor be spoiled by the destructive badger.

Towards sunset he left his work and turned to go home. He was very tired, but the thought of the nice supper of hot badger soup awaiting his return cheered him. The thought that the badger might get free and take revenge on the poor old woman never once came into his mind.

The badger meanwhile assumed the old woman's form, and as soon as he saw the old farmer approaching came out to greet him on the veranda of the little house, saying, "So you have come back at last. I have made the badger soup and have been waiting for you for a long time."

The old farmer quickly took off his straw sandals and sat down before his tiny dinner tray. The innocent man never even dreamed that it was not his wife but the badger who was waiting upon him, and asked at once for the soup. Then the badger suddenly transformed himself back to his natural form and cried out, "You wife-eating old man! Look out for the bones in the kitchen!"

Laughing loudly and derisively he escaped out of the house and ran away to his den in the hills. The old man was left behind alone. He could hardly believe what he had seen and heard.

Then when he understood the whole truth he was so scared and horrified that he fainted right away. After a while he came round and burst into tears. He cried loudly and bitterly. He rocked himself to and fro in his hopeless grief. It seemed too terrible to be real that his faithful old wife had been killed and cooked by the badger while he was working quietly in the fields, knowing nothing of what was going on at home, and congratulating himself on having once for all got rid of the wicked animal who had so often spoiled his fields. And oh! The horrible thought; he had very nearly drunk the soup which the creature had made of his poor old woman. "Oh dear, oh dear, oh dear!" he wailed aloud.

Now, not far away there lived in the same mountain a kind, good-natured old rabbit. He heard the old man crying and sobbing and at once set out to see what was the matter, and if there was anything he could do to help his neighbor.

The old man told him all that had happened. When the rabbit heard the story he was very angry at the wicked and deceitful badger, and told the old man to leave everything to him and he would avenge his wife's death. The farmer was at last comforted, and, wiping away his tears, thanked the rabbit for his goodness in coming to him in his distress.

The rabbit, seeing that the farmer was growing calmer, went back to his home to lay his plans for the punishment of the badger.

The next day the weather was fine, and the rabbit went out to find the badger. He was not to be seen in the woods or on the hillside or in the fields anywhere, so the rabbit went to his den and found the badger hiding there, for the animal had been afraid to show himself ever since he had escaped from the farmer's house, for fear of the old man's wrath.

The rabbit called out, "Why are you not out on such a beautiful day? Come out with me, and we will go and cut grass on the hills together."

The badger, never doubting but that the rabbit was his friend, willingly consented to go out with him, only too glad to get away from the neighborhood of the farmer and the fear of meeting him. The rabbit led the way miles away from their homes, out on the hills where the grass grew tall and thick and sweet. They both set to work to cut down as much as they could carry home, to store it up for their winter's food.

When they had each cut down all they wanted they tied it in bundles and then started homewards, each carrying his bundle of grass on his back. This time the rabbit made the badger go first.

When they had gone a little way the rabbit took out a flint and steel, and, striking it over the badger's back as he stepped along in front, set his bundle of grass on fire. The badger heard the flint striking, and asked, "What is that noise, 'Crack, crack'?"

"Oh, that is nothing," replied the rabbit; "I only said 'Crack, crack,' because this mountain is called Crackling Mountain."

The fire soon spread in the bundle of dry grass. The badger, hearing the crackle of the burning grass, asked, "What is that?"

"Now we have come to the 'Burning Mountain,'" answered the rabbit.

By this time the bundle was nearly burned out and all the hair had been burned off the badger's back. He now knew what had happened by the smell of the smoke of the burning grass. Screaming with pain the badger ran as fast as he could to his hole. The rabbit followed and found him lying on his bed groaning with pain.

"What an unlucky fellow you are!" said the rabbit. "I can't imagine how this happened! I will bring you some medicine which will heal your back quickly!"

The rabbit went away glad and smiling to think that the punishment upon the badger had already begun. He hoped that the badger would die of his burns, for he felt that nothing could be too bad for the animal, who was guilty of murdering a poor helpless old woman who had trusted him.

He went home and made an ointment by mixing some sauce and red pepper together. He carried this to the badger, but before putting it on he told him that it would cause him great pain, but that he must bear it patiently, because it was a very wonderful medicine for burns and scalds and such wounds.

The badger thanked him and begged him to apply it at once. But no language can describe the agony of the badger as soon as the red pepper had been pasted all over his sore back. He rolled over and over and howled loudly. The rabbit, looking on, felt that the farmer's wife was beginning to be avenged.

The badger was in bed for about a month; but at last, in spite of the red pepper application, his burns healed and he got well. When the rabbit saw that the badger was getting well, he thought of another plan by which he could compass the creature's death. So he went one day to pay the badger a visit and to congratulate him on his recovery.

During the conversation the rabbit mentioned that he was going fishing, and described how pleasant fishing was when the weather was fine and the sea smooth.

The badger listened with pleasure to the rabbit's account of the way he passed his time now, and forgot all his pains and his month's illness, and thought what fun it would be if he could go fishing too; so he asked the rabbit if he would take him the next time he went out to fish. This was just what the rabbit wanted, so he agreed.

Then he went home and built two boats, one of wood and the other of clay. At last they were both finished, and as the rabbit stood and looked at his work he felt that all his trouble would be well rewarded if his plan succeeded, and he could manage to kill the wicked badger now.

The day came when the rabbit had arranged to take the badger fishing. He kept the wooden boat himself and gave the badger the clay boat. The badger, who knew nothing about boats, was delighted with his new boat and thought how kind it was of the rabbit to give it to him. They both got into their boats and set out.

After going some distance from the shore the rabbit proposed that they should try their boats and see which one could go the quickest. The badger fell in with the proposal, and they both set to work to row as fast as they could for some time. In the middle of the race the badger found his boat going to pieces, for the water now began to soften the clay. He cried out in great fear to the rabbit to help him. But the rabbit answered that he was avenging the old woman's murder, and that this had been his intention all along, and that he was happy to think that the badger had at last met his deserts for all his evil crimes, and was to drown with no one to help him. Then he raised his oar and struck at the badger with all his strength till he fell with the sinking clay boat and was seen no more.

Thus at last he kept his promise to the old farmer. The rabbit now turned and rowed shorewards, and having landed and pulled his boat upon the beach, hurried back to tell the old farmer everything, and how the badger, his enemy, had been killed.

The old farmer thanked him with tears in his eyes. He said that till now he could never sleep at night or be at peace in the daytime, thinking of how his wife's death was unavenged, but from this time he would be able to sleep and eat as of old. He begged the rabbit to stay with him and share his home, so from this day the rabbit went to stay with the old farmer and they both lived together as good friends to the end of their days.

Source: "The Farmer and the Badger," Yei Theodora Ozaki. *Japanese Fairy Tales.* (New York: Grosset and Dunlap, 1906), pp. 42–48.

The Alligator and the Jackal

The following tale is originally from the Panchatantra, a work that according to Indian tradition dates from approximately 200 B.C.E. The tales in this collection are classified as fables, short fictional narratives in which animals or other nonhuman characters engage in interactions that illustrate a moral principle; this principle may be stated explicitly as a proverb. Seventeenth-century French author Jean de la Fontaine publicly acknowledged that the greater part of his tales were inspired by the Indian text. The fables of the Panchatantra continue to have an international impact. Indian Americans retain these fables as an element of their Asian cultural heritage.

A hungry Jackal once went down to the riverside in search of little crabs, bits of fish, and whatever else he could find for his dinner. Now it chanced that in this river there lived a great big Alligator, who, being also very hungry, would have been extremely glad to eat the Jackal.

The Jackal ran up and down, here and there, but for a long time could find nothing to eat. At last, close to where the Alligator was lying, among some tall bulrushes under the clear shallow water, he saw a little crab sidling along as fast as his legs could carry him. The Jackal was so hungry that when he saw this, he poked his paw into the water to try and catch the crab, when SNAP! the old Alligator caught hold of him. "Oh dear!" thought the Jackal to himself; "what can I do? this great big Alligator has caught my paw in his mouth, and in another minute he will drag me down by it under the water and kill me. My only chance is to make him think he has made a mistake." So he called out in a cheerful voice, "Clever Alligator, clever Alligator, to catch hold of a bulrush root instead of my paw! I hope you find it very tender." The Alligator, who was so buried among the bulrushes that he could hardly see, thought, on hearing this, "Dear me, how tiresome! I fancied I had caught hold of the Jackal's paw; but there he is, calling out in a cheerful voice; I suppose I must have seized a bulrush root instead, as he says." And he let the Jackal go.

The Jackal ran away as fast as he could, crying, "O wise Alligator, wise Alligator! So you let me go again!" Then the Alligator was very vexed, but the Jackal had run away too far to be caught. Next day the Jackal returned to the riverside to get his dinner, as before; but because he was very much afraid of the Alligator, he called out, "Whenever I go to look for my dinner, I see the nice little crabs peeping up through the mud, then I catch them and eat them. I wish I could see one now."

The Alligator, who was buried in the mud at the bottom of the river, heard every word. So he popped the little point of his snout above the water, thinking, "If I do but just show the tip of my nose, the Jackal will take me for a crab and put in his paw to catch me, and as soon as ever he does I'll gobble him up."

But no sooner did the Jackal see the little tip of the Alligator's nose than he called out, "Aha, my friend, there you are! No dinner for me in this part of the river then, I think." And so saying he ran further on, and fished for his dinner a long way from that place. The Alligator was very angry at missing his prey a second time, and determined not to let him escape again. So on the following day, when his little tormentor returned to the waterside, the Alligator hid himself close to the bank, in order to catch him if he could. Now the Jackal was rather afraid of going near the river, for he thought, "Perhaps this Alligator will catch me today." But yet, being hungry, he did not wish to go without his dinner; so to make all as safe as he could, he cried, "Where are all the little crabs gone? There is not one here, and I am so hungry; and generally, even when they are under water, one can see them going bubble, bubble, bubble, and all the little bubbles go pop! pop! pop!" On hearing this the Alligator, who was buried in the mud under the river-bank, thought, "I will pretend to be a little crab." And he began to blow, "Puff puff puff! Bubble, bubble, bubble!" and all the great big bubbles rushed to the surface of the river and burst there, and the waters eddied round and round like a whirlpool; and there was such a commotion when the huge monster began to blow bubbles in this way, that the Jackal saw very well who must be there, and he ran away as fast as he could, saying, "Thank you, kind Alligator, thank you; thank you. Indeed, I would not have come here had I known you were so close."

This enraged the Alligator extremely; it made him quite cross to think of being so often deceived by a little Jackal, and he said to himself, "I will be taken in no more. Next time I will be very cunning." So for a long time he waited and waited for the Jackal to return to the riverside; but the Jackal did not come, for he had thought to himself, "If matters go on in this way, I shall some day be caught, and eaten by the wicked old Alligator. I had better content myself with living on wild figs," and he went no more near the river, but stayed in the jungles and ate wild figs, and roots which he dug up with his paws.

When the Alligator found this out, he determined to try and catch the Jackal on land; so, going under the largest of the wild fig-trees, where the ground was covered with the fallen fruit, he collected a quantity of it together, and, burying himself under the great heap, waited for the Jackal to appear. But no sooner did the Jackal see this great heap of wild figs all collected together, than he thought, "That looks very like my friend the Alligator." And to discover if it was so or not he called out, "The juicy little wild figs I love to eat always tumble down from the tree, and roll here and there as the wind drives them; but this great heap of figs is quite still; these cannot be good figs, I will not eat any of them."—"Ho-ho!" thought the Alligator, "is that all? How suspicious this Jackal is! I will make the figs roll about a little then, and when he sees that he will doubtless come and eat them."

So the great beast shook himself, and all the heap of little figs went roll, roll, roll; some a mile this way, some a mile that, further than they had ever rolled before, or than the most blustering wind could have driven them!

Seeing this the Jackal scampered away, saying, "I am so much obliged to you, Alligator, for letting me know you are there, for indeed I should hardly have guessed it. You were so buried under that heap of figs." The Alligator hearing this was so angry that he ran after the Jackal, but the latter ran very, very fast away too quickly to be caught.

Then the Alligator said to himself, "I will not allow that little wretch to make fun of me another time, and then run away out of reach; I will show him that I can be more cunning than he fancies." And early the next morning he crawled as fast as he could to the Jackal's den (which was a hole in the side of a hill) and crept into it, and hid himself, waiting for the Jackal, who was out, to return home. But when the Jackal got near the place he looked about him and thought, "Dear me, the ground looks as if some heavy creature had been walking over it, and here are great clods of earth knocked down from each side of the door of my den as if a very big animal had been trying to squeeze himself through it. I certainly will not go inside until I know that all is safe there." So he called out, "Little house, pretty house, my sweet little house, why do you not give an answer when I call? If I come and all is safe and right, you always call out to me. Is anything wrong, that you do not speak?"

Then the Alligator, who was inside, thought, "If that is the case I had better call out, that he may fancy all is right in his house." And in as gentle a voice as he could, he said, "Sweet little Jackal."

At hearing these words the Jackal felt quite frightened, and thought to himself; "So the dreadful old Alligator is there! I must try to kill him if I can, for if I do not he will certainly catch and kill me some day." He therefore answered, "Thank you, my dear little house. I like to hear your pretty voice. I am coming in in a minute, but first I must collect firewood to cook my dinner." And he ran as fast as he could, and dragged all the dry branches and bits of stick he could find close up to the mouth of the den.

Meantime the Alligator inside kept as quiet as a mouse, but he could not help laughing a little to himself; as he thought, "So I have deceived this tiresome little Jackal at last. In a few minutes he will run in here, and then won't

I snap him up!" When the Jackal had gathered together all the sticks he could find, and put them round the mouth of his den, he set them alight and pushed them as far into it as possible. There was such a quantity of them that they soon blazed up into a great fire, and the smoke and flames filled the den and smothered the wicked old Alligator, and burnt him to death, while the little Jackal ran up and down outside, dancing for joy and singing—"How do you like my house, my friend? Is it nice and warm?

> Ding, dong! ding, dong! The Alligator is dying! ding, dong! ding, dong!
> He will trouble me no more. I have defeated my enemy!
> Ring a ting! ding a ting! ding, ding, dong!"

Source: "The Alligator and the Jackal," Mary Frere. *Old Deccan Days.* (London: J. Murray, 1868), pp. 234–238.

Rabbit's Eyes

Rabbit in the following Korean tale plays the role of the classic trick-ster. Although his curiosity puts him in peril, Rabbit uses his wits to escape from imminent death. The universal appeal of the trickster genre and the similarity of the Korean rabbit trickster to the rabbit tricksters of other ethnic cultures in the United States provides a favorable climate for the tale's preservation.

Once upon a time the king of the fishes fell ill, and no one knew what was the matter with him. All the doctors in the sea were called in, one after another, and not one of them could cure him.

Once when the fishes were talking about it, a turtle stuck its head out of a crack in a rock. "It is a pity," said the turtle, "that no one has ever thought of asking my advice. I could cure the king in a twinkling. All he has to do is to swallow the eye of a live rabbit, and he will become perfectly well again."

This the turtle said, not because he knew anything at all about the matter, but because he wished to appear wise before the fishes.

Now it so chanced that one of the fishes that heard him was the son of the king's councilor, and he swam straight home and told his father what he had heard the turtle say. The councilor told the king, and the king, who was feeling very ill that day, bade them bring the turtle to him immediately.

When the messengers told the turtle that the king wished to speak to him, the turtle was very much frightened. He drew his head and his tail into his shell and pretended that he was asleep, but in the end he was obliged to go with the messengers.

They soon reached the palace, and the turtle was taken immediately to where the king was. He was lying on a bed of seaweed and looking very ill indeed, and all his doctors were gathered round him.

The king turned his eyes toward the turtle, and spoke in a weak voice. "Tell me, friend, is it true that you said you could cure me?"

Yes, it was true.

"And that all I have to do is to swallow the eye of a live rabbit, and I will be well again?"

Yes, that was true too.

"Then go get a live rabbit and bring it here immediately, that I may be well."

When the turtle heard these words he was in despair. It did not seem at all likely that he could catch a rabbit and bring it down into the sea, but he was so much afraid of the king that he did not dare to explain this to him. He said nothing, but crawled away as soon as he could, wishing he could find some crack where he could hide himself and never be found again.

Suddenly he remembered he had once seen a rabbit frisking about on a hill not far from the seashore, and he determined to set out to find it. He crawled out of the sea and started up the hill. He climbed and he climbed, and after a while he came to the top, and there he sat down to rest.

Presently along came the rabbit, and it stopped to speak to him. "Good day," said the rabbit.

"Good day," said the turtle.

"And what are you doing so far away from the sea?" asked the rabbit.

"Oh, I only came up here to look about and see what the green world was like," answered the turtle.

"And what do you think of it, now you are here?"

"Oh, it's not so bad; but you ought to see the beautiful palaces and gardens we have down under the sea." The turtle began telling the rabbit about them, and he talked so long and said so many fine things about them, that the rabbit began to wish to see them for himself.

"Would it be very hard for me to live down under the water?" he asked.

"Oh, no," said the turtle. "It might be a little inconvenient at first, but that would not last long. If you like, I will take you on my back and carry you down to the bottom of the sea, and then you can see whether it is not all just as grand and beautiful as I have been telling you."

Well, the rabbit could not resist his curiosity, and he agreed to go with the turtle.

They went to the edge of the sea, and then the rabbit got on the turtle's back, and down they went through the water to the very bottom of the sea. The rabbit did not like it at first, but he soon grew used to it, and when he saw all the fine palaces and gardens that were there, he was filled with wonder.

The turtle took him directly to the palace of the king. There he bade the rabbit get down and wait awhile, and he promised that presently he would show him the king of all this magnificence. The rabbit was delighted and willingly agreed to wait there while the turtle went to announce him.

But while the turtle was away the rabbit heard two fishes talking in the room next to where he was. He was very inquisitive, so he cocked his ears forward and listened to what they were saying. What was his horror to find that they were talking about taking out his eyes and giving them to the king. The rabbit did not know what to do, nor how he was to escape from the dangerous position he was in.

Presently the turtle came back, and the chief councilor came with him, and immediately the rabbit began to talk. "Well," said he, "it all seems very fine here, and I am glad I came, but I wish now I had brought my own eyes with me so that I could see it better. You see, the eyes I have in my head now are only glass eyes. I am so afraid of getting my own eyes hurt or dusty that I generally keep them in a safe place, and wear these glass eyes instead. But if I had only known how much there would be to look at, I would certainly have brought my own eyes."

When the turtle and the councilor heard this, they were very much disappointed, for they believed the rabbit was speaking the truth, and that the eyes he had in his head at the time were only glass eyes.

"I will take you back to the shore," said the turtle, "and then you can go and get your real eyes and come back again, for there are many more things for you to see here, things more wonderful and beautiful than anything I have yet shown you."

Well, the rabbit was willing to do that, so he got upon the turtle's back, and the turtle swam up and up with him through the sea.

As soon as they reached the shore the rabbit leaped from the turtle's back, and away he went up the hill as fast as he could scamper, and he was glad enough to be out of that scrape, I can tell you. But the turtle waited, and he waited, and he waited, but the rabbit never did come back, and at last the turtle was obliged to go home without him.

As for the king of the fishes, if he ever got well, it was not the eye of a live rabbit that cured him; of that you may be sure.

Source: "The Rabbit's Eyes," Katharine Pyle. *Wonder Tales from Many Lands.* (London: George G. Harrap and Company, Ltd., 1910), pp. 108–113.

SOCIETY AND CONFLICT

How an Old Man Lost His Wen

A "wen" is a nonmalignant, though unsightly, tumor. Similar narratives of benign characters being healed of deformities (hunchbacks are common examples) by the good graces of "fairy folk" are found cross-culturally. The pairing of a decent character with a reprobate who seeks to benefit from the former's good work, but earns the punishment of a doubled affliction for his deceit, makes this a popular moral tale. This theme has led to the tale's retention in Japanese American tradition.

Many, many years ago there lived a good old man who had a wen like a tennis-ball growing out of his right cheek. This lump was a great disfigurement to the old man, and so annoyed him that for many years he spent all his time and money in trying to get rid of it. He tried everything he could think of. He consulted many doctors far and near, and took all kinds of medicines both internally and externally. But it was all of no use. The lump only grew bigger and bigger till it was nearly as big as his face, and in despair he gave up all hopes of ever losing it, and resigned himself to the thought of having to carry the lump on his face all his life.

One day the firewood gave out in his kitchen, so, as his wife wanted some at once, the old man took his ax and set out for the woods up among the hills not very far from his home. It was a fine day in the early autumn, and the old man enjoyed the fresh air and was in no hurry to get home. So the whole afternoon passed quickly while he was chopping wood, and he had collected a goodly pile to take back to his wife. When the day began to draw to a close, he turned his face homewards.

The old man had not gone far on his way down the mountain pass when the sky clouded and rain began to fall heavily. He looked about for some shelter, but there was not even a charcoal-burner's hut near. At last he espied a large hole in the hollow trunk of a tree. The hole was near the ground, so he crept in easily, and sat down in hopes that he had only been overtaken by a mountain shower, and that the weather would soon clear.

But much to the old man's disappointment, instead of clearing the rain fell more and more heavily, and finally a heavy thunderstorm broke over the mountain. The thunder roared so terrifically, and the heavens seemed to be so ablaze with lightning, that the old man could hardly believe himself to be alive. He thought that he must die of fright. At last, however, the sky cleared, and the whole country was aglow in the rays of the setting sun. The old man's spirits revived when he looked out at the beautiful twilight, and he was about to step out from his strange hiding-place in the hollow tree when the sound of what seemed like the approaching steps of several people caught his ear. He at once thought that his friends had come to look for him, and he was delighted at the idea of having some jolly companions with whom to walk home. But on looking out from the tree, what was his amazement to see, not his friends, but hundreds of demons coming towards the spot. The more he looked, the greater was his astonishment.

Some of these demons were as large as giants, others had great big eyes out of all proportion to the rest of their bodies, others again had absurdly long noses, and some had such big mouths that they seemed to open from ear to ear. All had horns growing on their foreheads. The old man was so surprised at what he saw that he lost his balance and fell out of the hollow tree. Fortunately for him the demons did not see him, as the tree was in the background. So he picked himself up and crept back into the tree.

While he was sitting there and wondering impatiently when he would be able to get home, he heard the sounds of gay music, and then some of the demons began to sing.

"What are these creatures doing?" said the old man to himself. "I will look out, it sounds very amusing."

On peeping out, the old man saw that the demon chief himself was actually sitting with his back against the tree in which he had taken refuge, and all the other demons were sitting round, some drinking and some dancing. Food and wine was spread before them on the ground, and the demons were evidently having a great entertainment and enjoying themselves immensely.

It made the old man laugh to see their strange antics. "How amusing this is!" laughed the old man to himself. "I am now quite old, but I have never seen anything so strange in all my life."

He was so interested and excited in watching all that the demons were doing, that he forgot himself and stepped out of the tree and stood looking on.

The demon chief was just taking a big cup of sake and watching one of the demons dancing. In a little while he said with a bored air, "Your dance is rather monotonous. I am tired of watching it. Isn't there any one amongst you all who can dance better than this fellow?"

Now the old man had been fond of dancing all his life, and was quite an expert in the art, and he knew that he could do much better than the demon.

"Shall I go and dance before these demons and let them see what a human being can do? It may be dangerous, for if I don't please them they may kill me!" said the old fellow to himself.

His fears, however, were soon overcome by his love of dancing. In a few minutes he could restrain himself no longer, and came out before the whole party of demons and began to dance at once. The old man, realizing that his life probably depended on whether he pleased these strange creatures or not, exerted his skill and wit to the utmost.

The demons were at first very surprised to see a man so fearlessly taking part in their entertainment, and then their surprise soon gave place to admiration.

"How strange!" exclaimed the horned chief. "I never saw such a skillful dancer before! He dances admirably!"

When the old man had finished his dance, the big demon said, "Thank you very much for your amusing dance. Now give us the pleasure of drinking a cup of wine with us," and with these words he handed him his largest wine-cup.

The old man thanked him very humbly, "I did not expect such kindness from your lordship. I fear I have only disturbed your pleasant party by my unskillful dancing."

"No, no," answered the big demon. "You must come often and dance for us. Your skill has given us much pleasure."

The old man thanked him again and promised to do so.

"Then will you come again tomorrow, old man?" asked the demon.

"Certainly, I will," answered the old man.

"Then you must leave some pledge of your word with us," said the demon.

"Whatever you like," said the old man.

"Now what is the best thing he can leave with us as a pledge?" asked the demon, looking round.

Then said one of the demon's attendants kneeling behind the chief, "The token he leaves with us must be the most important thing to him in his possession. I see the old man has a wen on his right cheek. Now mortal men consider such a wen very fortunate. Let my lord take the lump from the old man's right cheek, and he will surely come tomorrow, if only to get that back."

"You are very clever," said the demon chief, giving his horns an approving nod. Then the demon stretched out a hairy arm and claw-like hand, and took the great lump from the old man's right cheek. Strange to say, it came off as easily as a ripe plum from the tree at the demon's touch, and then the merry troop of demons suddenly vanished.

The old man was lost in bewilderment by all that had happened. He hardly knew for some time where he was. When he came to understand what had happened to him, he was delighted to find that the lump on his face, which had for so many years disfigured him, had really been taken away without any pain to himself. He put up his hand to feel if any scar remained, but found that his right cheek was as smooth as his left.

The sun had long set, and the young moon had risen like a silver crescent in the sky. The old man suddenly realized how late it was and began to hurry home. He patted his right cheek all the time, as if to make sure of his good fortune in having lost the wen. He was so happy that he found it impossible to walk quietly; he ran and danced the whole way home.

He found his wife very anxious, wondering what had happened to make him so late. He soon told her all that had passed since he left home that afternoon. She was quite as happy as her husband when he showed her that the ugly lump had disappeared from his face, for in her youth she had prided herself on his good looks, and it had been a daily grief to her to see the horrid growth.

Now next door to this good old couple there lived a wicked and disagreeable old man. He, too, had for many years been troubled with the growth of a wen on his left cheek, and he, too, had tried all manner of things to get rid of it, but in vain.

He heard at once, through the servant, of his neighbor's good luck in losing the lump on his face, so he called that very evening and asked his friend to tell him everything that concerned the loss of it. The good old man told his disagreeable neighbor all that had happened to him. He described the place where he would find the hollow tree in which to hide, and advised him to be on the spot in the late afternoon towards the time of sunset.

The old neighbor started out the very next afternoon, and after hunting about for some time, came to the hollow tree just as his friend had described. Here he hid himself and waited for the twilight.

Just as he had been told, the band of demons came at that hour and held a feast with dance and song. When this had gone on for some time the chief of the demons looked around and said, "It is now time for the old man to come as he promised us. Why doesn't he come?"

When the second old man heard these words he ran out of his hiding-place in the tree and, kneeling down before the oni, said, "I have been waiting for a long time for you to speak!"

"Ah, you are the old man of yesterday," said the demon chief. "Thank you for coming, you must dance for us soon."

The old man now stood up and opened his fan and began to dance. But he had never learned to dance, and knew nothing about the necessary gestures and different positions. He thought that anything would please the demons, so he just hopped about, waving his arms and stamping his feet, imitating as well as he could any dancing he had ever seen.

The oni were very dissatisfied at this exhibition, and said amongst themselves, "How badly he dances today!"

Then to the old man the demon chief said, "Your performance today is quite different from the dance of yesterday. We don't wish to see any more of such dancing. We will give you back the pledge you left with us. You must go away at once." With these words he took out from a fold of his dress the lump which he had taken from the face of the old man who had danced so well the day before, and threw it at the right cheek of the old man who stood before him. The lump immediately attached itself to his cheek as firmly as if it had grown there always, and all attempts to pull it off were useless. The wicked old man, instead of losing the lump on his left cheek as he had hoped, found to his dismay that he had but added another to his right cheek in his attempt to get rid of the first.

He put up first one hand and then the other to each side of his face to make sure if he were not dreaming a horrible nightmare. No, sure enough there was now a great wen on the right side of his face as on the left. The demons had all disappeared, and there was nothing for him to do but to return home. He was a pitiful sight, for his face, with the two large lumps, one on each side, looked just like a Japanese gourd.

Source: "How an Old Man Lost His Wen," Yei Theodora Ozaki. *Japanese Fairy Tales.* (New York: Grosset & Dunlap Publishers, 1903), pp. 282–292.

Datto Somacuel

*Filipino legend states that Somacuel (sometimes spelled as "Sumakwel")
was one of the seven (according to some versions ten) dattos (also, datus,
"village chiefs") who left Borneo in order to establish a precolonial society in the Philippine Islands. While the legend warns against the dangers
of rage and infidelity, its primary contemporary value is that the tale
serves as a link to the earliest period in Filipino history.*

Datto Somacuel was one of the seven chiefs who, coming from Borneo
many years before the Spaniards conquered these islands, settled the Island
of Panay. He lived in Sinaragan, a town near San Joaquin, in the southern
part of Iloilo Province. His wife's name was Capinangan.

Somacuel went every morning to the seashore to watch his slaves fish with
the sinchoro, or net. One day they caught many fishes, and Somacuel
commanded them, "Spread the fish to dry, and take care that the crows do
not eat them up."

A slave answered: "Sir, if your treasure inside the house is stolen by the
crows, how do you expect those out of doors to be kept safe?" This was said
with a certain intonation that made Somacuel conjecture that there was a
hidden meaning in it.

"What do you mean by that?" he asked.

"Sir, I have to inform you of something that I should have told you long
ago. Do not reprove me if I have been backward in telling you of the injury
done you by your wife. It was due to my desire to get complete proofs of the
truth of my statement."

"End at once your tedious narrative!" said the datto, "What did my
wife do?"

"Sir," answered the slave, "she deceives you shamefully. She loves
Gorong-Gorong, who is at this very moment in your house jesting at your
absence."

"Alas!" said Somacuel, "if this be true he shall pay well for his boldness."

The chief hurried home, intending to surprise the offenders. He carried a
fish called ampahan in a bamboo tube full of water, going around by a secret
way, so as not to be seen. On reaching home he went up into the attic to
observe what was going on, and found that his informant had told the truth.

Gorong-Gorong and Capinangan were engaged in an affectionate dialogue. Involuntarily Somacuel spilled some of the water down, and, fearing that he would be discovered, seized a spear that was hidden in the attic and, dropping it down as if it had fallen accidentally, dexterously ran Gorong-Gorong through the body, killing him instantly.

"Oh, Diva!" exclaimed Capinangan, kneeling beside the inert corpse, "How shall I be able to take it away without being discovered by Somacuel?"

Somacuel, who had not been seen at all, stayed quietly above, watching what Capinangan would do. Capinangan did not suspect that her husband was there, as he usually did not come home before nightfall. She tried to take the corpse out for burial, but could not carry the heavy body of her unfortunate lover. She must conceal it in some way, and it was dangerous for her to call for aid, lest she might be betrayed to her husband. So she took a knife and cut the body into pieces so that she could take them out and bury them under the house.

After this task was done she managed to wash the blood up. She became tranquil for a moment, believing she would never be discovered. Somacuel, however, had observed all, and he formed a plan for punishing his wife as she deserved. When everything seemed to be calm he crept down, doing his best not to be seen. At the door he called his wife by name. Capinangan was afraid, but concealed her fear with a smile. "Capinangan," said her husband, "cut this fish in pieces and cook it for me."

Capinangan was astonished at this command, because she had never before been treated in this way. They had many slaves to perform such tasks.

"You know I cannot," she said.

"Why not?" asked her husband.

"Because I have never learned how to cut a fish in pieces nor to cook it," she replied.

"I am astonished that you don't know how to cut, after seeing that cutting is your favorite occupation," said Somacuel.

Capinangan then did not doubt that her husband knew what she had done, so she did as he had bidden.

When dinner was ready the husband and wife ate it, but without speaking to each other. After the meal, Somacuel told his wife that he had seen all and should punish her severely. Capinangan said nothing. A guilty person has no argument with which to defend himself. Somacuel ordered his servants to throw Capinangan into the sea. At that time the chief's will was law. Neither pleadings nor tears softened his hard heart, and Capinangan was carried down to the sea and thrown in.

Time passed by; Somacuel each day grew sadder and gloomier. He would have been willing now to forgive his wife, but it was too late.

He said to his slaves: "Prepare a banca [type of Filipino boat] for me, that I may sail from place to place to amuse myself."

So one pleasant morning a banca sailed from Sinaragan, going southward. Somacuel did not intend to go to any definite place, but drifted at the mercy of wind and current. He amused himself by singing during the voyage.

One day the crew descried land at a distance. "Sir," they said, "that land is Cagayan. Let us go there to get oysters and crane's eggs." To this their master agreed, and upon anchoring off the coast he prepared to visit the place.

Oh, what astonishment he felt, as he saw, peeping out of the window of a house, a woman whose appearance resembled in great measure that of Capinangan! He would have run to embrace her, had he not remembered that Capinangan was dead. He was informed that the woman was named Aloyan. He began to pay court to her, and in a few weeks she became his wife.

Somacuel was happy, for his wife was very affectionate. Aloyan, on her part, did not doubt that her husband loved her sincerely, so she said to him: "My dear Somacuel, I will no longer deceive you. I am the very woman whom you caused to be thrown into the sea. I am Capinangan. I clung to a log in the water and was carried to this place, where I have lived ever since."

"Oh," said Somacuel, "pardon me for the harshness with which I meant to punish you."

"Let us forget what is passed," said Capinangan. "I deserved it, after all."

So they returned to Sinaragan, where they lived together happily for many years.

Source: "Datto Somacuel," Berton L. Maxfield and W.H. Millington, "Visayan Folk-Tales, II." *Journal of American Folklore* 20 (1907): 89–103, pp. 93–95.

Maria and the Seven Princes

According to some commentators, the Cinderella tale type is the most widely distributed folktale in the world. This Filipino variant of the tale is more gruesome than the versions found in contemporary U.S. popular culture. In many ways, it is closer to the dark European renderings of the tale (the Grimms' version of "Ash Girl," for example). However, good still triumphs over evil as in the more familiar contemporary variants of the story. Localization is apparent in the use of a crab as the heroine's supernatural helper and in the lukban tree, which grows from the crab's shell.

There were once a man and his wife who had one daughter who was very beautiful, named Maria. The man fell in love with a widow who had three children. One day while he and his wife were on the river in a boat, he pushed her out and she was drowned. Then he married the other woman, who was as wicked as he.

Poor Maria, with all her beauty, became the household drudge, condemned to do all the dirty work, and forever black with soot. One day while she was washing by the riverbank there came from the river a large female crab, which said to her, "Take me home, cook me, but though the others may eat me you must not. Save only my shell and bury that in the garden."

All this Maria did. Although the others asked her why she would not eat the crab, she would not taste it, and she buried the shell in the garden. From the shell there grew a beautiful *lukban* [grapefruit] tree, which had three great fruits.

One Sunday she bathed herself, washed the soot from her face and went to the *lukban* tree. Opening one of the fruits, she took out a magnificent dress with jewels and a beautiful horse. Arraying herself, she placed herself on the horse's back and was carried to the church.

The king was there and wished to speak with the beautiful princess, for by her dress she must be such; but as soon as the priest had pronounced the benediction she slipped out the door. The king ordered all his soldiers to follow, but so swift was her horse that all they could bring him was one of the little slippers that fell from the foot of the girl as she rode. With this the king could not be content, and so he ordered that all women with little feet be brought to him to try on the shoe.

The soldiers went here, there, and everywhere looking for little feet, but the shoe would fit none. At last they came to the house of Maria's father. Now Maria had a very small foot while those of her stepsisters were large, so the stepmother wrapped Maria in an old mat and put her above on the rafters, telling her that she must not move. The soldiers searched the house.

Said one of them, "Surely that is some one wrapped in that mat."

"Oh, no," said the stepmother, "that is only a bundle of old rags." But the soldier pricked it with his sword, which forced poor Maria to cry out. The soldiers then had her wash her face and were astonished at her beauty. So they took her to the king and the shoe fitted exactly.

The king married her with great feasting and pomp, and they lived very happily for a while. But the duties of state carried the king to a distant city, and as he was expecting the birth of an heir, he gave orders that she should be carefully watched that no enemy should reach her.

Finally the heir was born, but instead of one, there were seven handsome little princes. But the wicked stepmother, by some artifice, gained access to the chamber and there substituted seven newborn little puppies, with their eyes yet closed. The news that the queen had brought forth puppies was carried to the king, and he gave orders that they and their mother should be well treated but that they should be placed in a room outside of the palace walls, and that none should be allowed to see them.

The real princes, so wickedly stolen, were carried by the stepmother in a basket to the mountains and there exposed. But by a miracle they survived, and when they had grown into handsome boys their nurse sent them to town to church. As they went by the room where their mother was imprisoned they all turned and bowed most courteously to the occupant.

At the church they attracted much attention, and by the king's order they were bidden to dinner at the royal table. But by their nurse's directions they were not to eat unless their mother sat at the table too. The king, willing to oblige such handsome boys, all dressed exactly alike, and alike in face and manner, ordered that his wife be released and given a place at the table.

So the boys seated themselves, three on one side of the queen and four on the other, and behold a miracle, for the queen's breasts filled with milk, which streamed to the mouths of the seven boys. Then the king learned of the deception that had been put upon him, and he ordered that the wicked stepmother be taken out and dragged to pieces by horses, and it was done.

As for the king, Queen Maria, and the seven princes, long and happily they lived and blessed they died.

Source: Fletcher Gardner and W.W. Newell. "Filipino (Tagalog) Versions of Cinderella," *Journal of American Folklore* 19 (1906): 265–70, pp. 270–272.

The Tongue-Cut Sparrow

This tale is said to be almost universally known in the Japanese American community of the West Coast. It is considered by community members to be integral to the traditional culture transmitted to the American context. Little, if any, localization is seen in the U.S. variants of this tale. Unlike many of the tales preserved in this tradition, the wicked character is reformed by her experience rather than destroyed.

Long, long ago in Japan there lived an old man and his wife. The old man was a good, kindhearted, hardworking old fellow, but his wife was a regular crosspatch, who spoiled the happiness of her home by her scolding tongue. She was always grumbling about something from morning to night. The old man had for a long time ceased to take any notice of her crossness. He was out most of the day at work in the fields, and as he had no child, for his amusement when he came home, he kept a tame sparrow. He loved the little bird just as much as if she had been his child.

When he came back at night after his hard day's work in the open air it was his only pleasure to pet the sparrow, to talk to her and to teach her little tricks, which she learned very quickly. The old man would open her cage and let her fly about the room, and they would play together. Then when suppertime came, he always saved some tidbits from his meal with which to feed his little bird.

Now one day the old man went out to chop wood in the forest, and the old woman stopped at home to wash clothes. The day before, she had made some starch, and now when she came to look for it, it was all gone; the bowl which she had filled full yesterday was quite empty.

While she was wondering who could have used or stolen the starch, down flew the pet sparrow, and bowing her little feathered head, a trick which she had been taught by her master, the pretty bird chirped and said: "It is I who have taken the starch. I thought it was some food put out for me in that basin, and I ate it all. If I have made a mistake I beg you to forgive me! Tweet, tweet, tweet!"

You see from this that the sparrow was a truthful bird, and the old woman ought to have been willing to forgive her at once when she asked her pardon so nicely. But not so.

The old woman had never loved the sparrow, and had often quarreled with her husband for keeping what she called a dirty bird about the house, saying that it only made extra work for her. Now she was only too delighted to have some cause of complaint against the pet. She scolded and even cursed the poor little bird for her bad behavior, and not content with using these harsh, unfeeling words, in a fit of rage she seized the sparrow who all this time had spread out her wings and bowed her head before the old woman, to show how sorry she was and fetched the scissors and cut off the poor little bird's tongue.

"I suppose you took my starch with that tongue! Now you may see what it is like to go without it!" And with these dreadful words she drove the bird away, not caring in the least what might happen to it and without the smallest pity for its suffering, so unkind was she!

The old woman, after she had driven the sparrow away, made some more rice-paste, grumbling all the time at the trouble, and after starching all her clothes, spread the things on boards to dry in the sun.

In the evening the old man came home. As usual, on the way back he looked forward to the time when he should reach his gate and see his pet come flying and chirping to meet him, ruffling out her feathers to show her joy, and at last coming to rest on his shoulder. But tonight the old man was very disappointed, for not even the shadow of his dear sparrow was to be seen.

He quickened his steps, hastily drew off his straw sandals, and stepped on to the veranda. Still no sparrow was to be seen. He now felt sure that his wife, in one of her cross tempers, had shut the sparrow up in its cage. So he called her and said anxiously: "Where is Suzume San (Miss Sparrow) today?"

The old woman pretended not to know at first, and answered: "Your sparrow? I am sure I don't know. Now I come to think of it, I haven't seen her all the afternoon. I shouldn't wonder if the ungrateful bird had flown away and left you after all your petting!"

But at last, when the old man gave her no peace, but asked her again and again, insisting that she must know what had happened to his pet, she confessed all. She told him crossly how the sparrow had eaten the rice-paste she had specially made for starching her clothes, and how when the sparrow had confessed to what she had done, in great anger she had taken her scissors and cut out her tongue, and how finally she had driven the bird away and forbidden her to return to the house again.

Then the old woman showed her husband the sparrow's tongue, saying: "Here is the tongue I cut off! Horrid little bird, why did it eat all my starch?"

"How could you be so cruel? Oh! How could you so cruel?" was all that the old man could answer. He was too kindhearted to punish his shrew of a wife, but he was terribly distressed at what had happened to his poor little sparrow.

"What a dreadful misfortune for my poor Suzume San to lose her tongue!" he said to himself. "She won't be able to chirp any more, and surely the pain of the cutting of it out in that rough way must have made her ill! Is there nothing to be done?"

The old man shed many tears after his cross wife had gone to sleep. While he wiped away the tears with the sleeve of his cotton robe, a bright thought comforted him. He would go and look for the sparrow on the morrow. Having decided this he was able to go to sleep at last.

The next morning he rose early, as soon as ever the day broke, and snatching a hasty breakfast, started out over the hills and through the woods, stopping at every clump of bamboos to cry, "Where, oh where does my tongue-cut sparrow stay? Where, oh where, does my tongue-cut sparrow stay?"

He never stopped to rest for his noonday meal, and it was far on in the afternoon when he found himself near a large bamboo wood. Bamboo groves are the favorite haunts of sparrows, and there sure enough at the edge of the wood he saw his own dear sparrow waiting to welcome him. He could hardly believe his eyes for joy, and ran forward quickly to greet her. She bowed her little head and went through a number of the tricks her master had taught her, to show her pleasure at seeing her old friend again, and, wonderful to relate, she could talk as of old. The old man told her how sorry he was for all that had happened, and inquired after her tongue, wondering how she could speak so well without it. Then the sparrow opened her beak and showed him that a new tongue had grown in place of the old one, and begged him not to think any more about the past, for she was quite well now. Then the old man knew that his sparrow was a fairy, and no common bird. It would be difficult to exaggerate the old man's rejoicing now.

He forgot all his troubles, he forgot even how tired he was, for he had found his lost sparrow, and instead of being ill and without a tongue as he had feared and expected to find her, she was well and happy and with a new tongue, and without a sign of the ill-treatment she had received from his wife. And above all she was a fairy.

The sparrow asked him to follow her, and flying before him she led him to a beautiful house in the heart of the bamboo grove. The old man was utterly astonished when he entered the house to find what a beautiful place it was. It was built of the whitest wood, the soft cream colored mats which took the place of carpets were the finest he had ever seen, and the cushions that the sparrow brought out for him to sit on were made of the finest silk and crape. Beautiful vases and lacquer boxes adorned the alcoves of every room.

The sparrow led the old man to the place of honor, and then, taking her place at a humble distance, she thanked him with many polite bows for all the kindness he had shown her for many long years.

Then the Lady Sparrow, as we will now call her, introduced all her family to the old man. This done, her daughters, robed in dainty crape gowns, brought in on beautiful old-fashioned trays a feast of all kinds of delicious foods, till the old man began to think he must be dreaming. In the middle of the dinner some of the sparrow's daughters performed a wonderful dance, called the "Suzume-odori" or the "Sparrow's dance," to amuse the guest.

Never had the old man enjoyed himself so much. The hours flew by too quickly in this lovely spot, with all these fairy sparrows to wait upon him and to feast him and to dance before him.

But the night came on and the darkness reminded him that he had a long way to go and must think about taking his leave and return home. He thanked his kind hostess for her splendid entertainment, and begged her for his sake to forget all she had suffered at the hands of his cross old wife. He told the Lady Sparrow that it was a great comfort and happiness to him to find her in such a beautiful home and to know that she wanted for nothing. It was his anxiety to know how she fared and what had really happened to her that had led him to seek her. Now he knew that all was well he could return home with a light heart. If ever she wanted him for anything she had only to send for him and he would come at once.

The Lady Sparrow begged him to stay and rest several days and enjoy the change, but the old man said he must return to his old wife who would probably be cross at his not coming home at the usual time and to his work, and therefore, much as he wished to do so, he could not accept her kind invitation. But now that he knew where the Lady Sparrow lived he would come to see her whenever he had the time.

When the Lady Sparrow saw that she could not persuade the old man to stay longer, she gave an order to some of her servants, and they at once brought in two boxes, one large and the other small. These were placed before the old man, and the Lady Sparrow asked him to choose whichever he liked for a present, which she wished to give him.

The old man could not refuse this kind proposal, and he chose the smaller box, saying, "I am now too old and feeble to carry the big and heavy box. As you are so kind as to say that I may take whichever I like, I will choose the small one, which will be easier for me to carry."

Then the sparrows all helped him put it on his back and went to the gate to see him off, bidding him good-by with many bows and entreating him to come again whenever he had the time. Thus the old man and his pet sparrow separated quite happily, the sparrow showing not the least ill-will for all the unkindness she had suffered at the hands of the old wife. Indeed, she only felt sorrow for the old man who had to put up with it all his life.

When the old man reached home he found his wife even crosser than usual, for it was late on in the night and she had been waiting up for him for a long time.

"Where have you been all this time?" she asked in a big voice. "Why do you come back so late?"

The old man tried to pacify her by showing her the box of presents he had brought back with him, and then he told her of all that had happened to him, and how wonderfully he had been entertained at the sparrow's house.

"Now let us see what is in the box," said the old man, not giving her time to grumble again.

"You must help me open it." And they both sat down before the box and opened it.

To their utter astonishment they found the box filled to the brim with gold and silver coins and many other precious things. The mats of their little cottage fairly glittered as they took out the things one by one and put them down and handled them over and over again. The old man was overjoyed at the sight of the riches that were now his. Beyond his brightest expectations was the sparrow's gift, which would enable him to give up work and live in ease and comfort the rest of his days.

He said, "Thanks to my good little sparrow! Thanks to my good little sparrow!" many times.

But the old woman, after the first moments of surprise and satisfaction at the sight of the gold and silver were over, could not suppress the greed of her wicked nature. She now began to reproach the old man for not having brought home the big box of presents, for in the innocence of his heart he had told her how he had refused the large box of presents which the sparrows had offered him, preferring the smaller one because it was light and easy to carry home.

"You silly old man," said she, "Why did you not bring the large box? Just think what we have lost. We might have had twice as much silver and gold as this. You are certainly an old fool!" she screamed, and then went to bed as angry as she could be.

The old man now wished that he had said nothing about the big box, but it was too late; the greedy old woman, not contented with the good luck which had so unexpectedly befallen them and which she so little deserved, made up her mind, if possible, to get more.

Early the next morning she got up and made the old man describe the way to the sparrow's house. When he saw what was in her mind he tried to keep her from going, but it was useless. She would not listen to one word he said. It is strange that the old woman did not feel ashamed of going to see the sparrow after the cruel way she had treated her in cutting off her tongue in a fit of rage. But her greed to get the big box made her forget everything else. It did not even enter her thoughts that the sparrows might be angry with her as, indeed, they were and might punish her for what she had done.

Ever since the Lady Sparrow had returned home in the sad plight in which they had first found her, weeping and bleeding from the mouth, her whole family and relations had done little else but speak of the cruelty of the old woman. "How could she," they asked each other, "inflict such a heavy punishment for such a trifling offense as that of eating some rice-paste by mistake?"

They all loved the old man who was so kind and good and patient under all his troubles, but the old woman they hated, and they determined, if ever they had the chance, to punish her as she deserved. They had not long to wait.

After walking for some hours the old woman had at last found the bamboo grove which she had made her husband carefully describe, and now she stood before it crying out, "Where is the tongue-cut sparrow's house? Where is the tongue-cut sparrow's house?"

At last she saw the eaves of the house peeping out from amongst the bamboo foliage. She hastened to the door and knocked loudly.

When the servants told the Lady Sparrow that her old mistress was at the door asking to see her, she was somewhat surprised at the unexpected visit, after all that had taken place, and she wondered not a little at the boldness of the old woman in venturing to come to the house. The Lady Sparrow, however, was a polite bird, and so she went out to greet the old woman, remembering that she had once been her mistress.

The old woman intended, however, to waste no time in words, she went right to the point, without the least shame, and said: "You need not trouble to entertain me as you did my old man. I have come myself to get the box which he so stupidly left behind. I shall soon take my leave if you will give me the big box that is all I want!"

The Lady Sparrow at once consented, and told her servants to bring out the big box. The old woman eagerly seized it and hoisted it on her back, and without even stopping to thank the Lady Sparrow began to hurry homewards.

The box was so heavy that she could not walk fast, much less run, as she would have liked to do, so anxious was she to get home and see what was inside the box, but she had often to sit down and rest herself by the way.

While she was staggering along under the heavy load, her desire to open the box became too great to be resisted. She could wait no longer, for she supposed this big box to be full of gold and silver and precious jewels like the small one her husband had received.

At last this greedy and selfish old woman put down the box by the wayside and opened it carefully, expecting to gloat her eyes on a mine of wealth. What she saw, however, so terrified her that she nearly lost her senses. As soon as she lifted the lid, a number of horrible and frightful looking demons bounced out of the box and surrounded her as if they intended to kill her. Not even in nightmares had she ever seen such horrible creatures as her much-coveted box contained. A demon with one huge eye right in the middle of its forehead came and glared at her, monsters with gaping mouths looked as if they would devour her, a huge snake coiled and hissed about her, and a big frog hopped and croaked towards her.

The old woman had never been so frightened in her life, and ran from the spot as fast as her quaking legs would carry her, glad to escape alive. When she reached home she fell to the floor and told her husband with tears all that had happened to her, and how she had been nearly killed by the demons in the box.

Then she began to blame the sparrow, but the old man stopped her at once, saying: "Don't blame the sparrow, it is your wickedness which has at last met with its reward. I only hope this may be a lesson to you in the future!"

The old woman said nothing more, and from that day she repented of her cross, unkind ways, and by degrees became a good old woman, so that her husband hardly knew her to be the same person, and they spent their last days together happily, free from want or care, spending carefully the treasure the old man had received from his pet, the tongue-cut sparrow.

Source: "The Tongue-Cut Sparrow," Yei Theodora Ozaki. *Japanese Fairy Tales.* (New York: Grosset and Dunlap, 1906), pp. 11–24.

The Quarrel of the Monkey and the Crab

The monkey in the following tale is a trickster character of the same malicious type as the tanuki in "The Farmer and the Badger" (pp. 77–81). These sinister exploiters were preserved in the Japanese American repertoire to serve as models of antisocial behavior. The young crab, on the other hand, in pursuing his goal of avenging his father's death, upholds the ideal of filial piety (respect for one's parents) that the community hoped to instill in younger generations.

Long, long ago, one bright autumn day in Japan, it happened that a pink-faced monkey and a yellow crab were playing together along the bank of a river. As they were running about, the crab found a rice-dumpling and the monkey a persimmon-seed.

The crab picked up the rice-dumpling and showed it to the monkey, saying, "Look what a nice thing I have found!"

Then the monkey held up his persimmon-seed and said: " I also have found something good! Look!"

Now though the monkey is always very fond of persimmon fruit, he had no use for the seed he had just found. The persimmon-seed is as hard and uneatable as a stone. He, therefore, in his greedy nature, felt very envious of the crab's nice dumpling, and he proposed an exchange. The crab naturally did not see why he should give up his prize for a hard stone-like seed, and would not consent to the monkey's proposition.

Then the cunning monkey began to persuade the crab, saying: "How unwise you are not to think of the future! Your rice-dumpling can be eaten now, and is certainly much bigger than my seed; but if you sow this seed in the ground it will soon grow and become a great tree in a few years, and bear an abundance of fine ripe persimmons year after year. If only I could show it to you then with the yellow fruit hanging on its branches!

Of course, if you don't believe me I shall sow it myself; though I am sure, later on, you will be very sorry that you did not take my advice."

The simple-minded crab could not resist the monkey's clever persuasion. He at last gave in and consented to the monkey's proposal, and the exchange was made. The greedy monkey soon gobbled up the dumpling, and with great reluctance gave up the persimmon-seed to the crab.

He would have liked to keep that too, but he was afraid of making the crab angry and of being pinched by his sharp scissor-like claws. They then separated, the monkey going home to his forest trees and the crab to his stones along the riverside. As soon as the crab reached home he put the persimmon-seed in the ground as the monkey had told him.

In the following spring the crab was delighted to see the shoot of a young tree push its way up through the ground. Each year it grew bigger, till at last it blossomed one spring, and in the following autumn bore some fine large persimmons. Among the broad smooth green leaves the fruit hung like golden balls, and as they ripened they mellowed to a deep orange. It was the little crab's pleasure to go out day by day and sit in the sun and put out his long eyes in the same way as a snail puts out its horn, and watch the persimmons ripening to perfection.

"How delicious they will be to eat!" he said to himself.

At last, one day, he knew the persimmons must be quite ripe and he wanted very much to taste one. He made several attempts to climb the tree, in the vain hope of reaching one of the beautiful persimmons hanging above him; but he failed each time, for a crab's legs are not made for climbing trees but only for running along the ground and over stones, both of which he can do most cleverly. In his dilemma he thought of his old playmate the monkey, who, he knew, could climb trees better than any one else in the world.

He determined to ask the monkey to help him, and set out to find him.

Running crab-fashion up the stony river bank, over the pathways into the shadowy forest, the crab at last found the monkey taking an afternoon nap in his favorite pine-tree, with his tail curled tight around a branch to prevent him from falling off in his dreams. He was soon wide awake, however, when he heard himself called, and eagerly listening to what the crab told him. When he heard that the seed which he had long ago exchanged for a rice-dumpling had grown into a tree and was now bearing good fruit, he was delighted, for he at once devised a cunning plan which would give him all the persimmons for himself.

He consented to go with the crab to pick the fruit for him. When they both reached the spot, the monkey was astonished to see what a fine tree had sprung from the seed, and with what a number of ripe persimmons the branches were loaded.

He quickly climbed the tree and began to pluck and eat, as fast as he could, one persimmon after another. Each time he chose the best and ripest he could find, and went on eating till he could eat no more. Not one would he give to the poor hungry crab waiting below, and when he had finished there was little but the hard, unripe fruit left.

You can imagine the feelings of the poor crab after waiting patiently, for so long as he had done, for the tree to grow and the fruit to ripen, when he saw the monkey devouring all the good persimmons. He was so disappointed that he ran round and round the tree calling to the monkey to remember his promise. The monkey at first took no notice of the crab's complaints, but at last he picked out the hardest, greenest persimmon he could find and aimed it at the crab's head. The persimmon is as hard as stone when it is unripe.

The monkey's missile struck home and the crab was sorely hurt by the blow. Again and again, as fast as he could pick them, the monkey pulled off the hard persimmons and threw them at the defenseless crab till he dropped dead, covered with wounds all over his body. There he lay a pitiful sight at the foot of the tree he had himself planted.

When the wicked monkey saw that he had killed the crab he ran away from the spot as fast as he could, in fear and trembling, like a coward as he was.

Now the crab had a son who had been playing with a friend not far from the spot where this sad work had taken place. On the way home he came across his father dead, in a most dreadful condition his head was smashed and his shell broken in several places, and around his body lay the unripe persimmons which had done their deadly work. At this dreadful sight the poor young crab sat down and wept.

But when he had wept for some time he told himself that this crying would do no good; it was his duty to avenge his father's murder, and this he determined to do. He looked about for some clue which would lead him to discover the murderer. Looking up at the tree he noticed that the best fruit had gone, and that all around lay bits of peel and numerous seeds strewn on the ground as well as the unripe persimmons which had evidently been thrown at his father. Then he understood that the monkey was the murderer, for he now remembered that his father had once told him the story of the rice-dumpling and the persimmon-seed. The young crab knew that monkeys liked persimmons above all other fruit, and he felt sure that his greed for the coveted fruit had been the cause of the old crab's death. Alas!

He at first thought of going to attack the monkey at once, for he burned with rage. Second thoughts, however, told him that this was useless, for the monkey was an old and cunning animal and would be hard to overcome. He must meet cunning with cunning and ask some of his friends to help him, for he knew it would be quite out of his power to kill him alone.

The young crab set out at once to call on the mortar, his father's old friend, and told him of all that had happened. He besought the mortar with tears to help him avenge his father's death. The mortar was very sorry when he heard the woeful tale and promised at once to help the young crab punish the monkey to death. He warned him that he must be very careful in what he did, for the monkey was a strong and cunning enemy. The mortar now sent to fetch the bee and the chestnut (also the crab's old friends) to consult them about the matter. In a short time the bee and the chestnut arrived. When they were told all the details of the old crab's death and of the monkey's wickedness and greed, they both gladly consented to help the young crab in his revenge.

After talking for a long time as to the ways and means of carrying out their plans they separated, and Mr. Mortar went home with the young crab to help him bury his poor father.

While all this was taking place the monkey was congratulating himself (as the wicked often do before their punishment comes upon them) on all he had done so neatly. He thought it quite a fine thing that he had robbed his friend of all his ripe persimmons and then that he had killed him.

Still, smile as hard as he might, he could not banish altogether the fear of the consequences should his evil deeds be discovered. If he were found out (and he told himself that this could not be for he had escaped unseen) the crab's family would be sure to bear him hatred and seek to take revenge on him. So he would not go out, and kept himself at home for several days. He found this kind of life, however, extremely dull, accustomed as he was to the free life of the woods, and at last he said: "No one knows that it was I who killed the crab! I am sure that the old thing breathed his last before I left him. Dead crabs have no mouths! Who is there to tell that I am the murderer? Since no one knows, what is the use of shutting myself up and brooding over the matter? What is done cannot be undone!"

With this he wandered out into the crab settlement and crept about as slyly as possible near the crab's house and tried to hear the neighbors' gossip round about. He wanted to find out what the crabs were saying about their chief's death, for the old crab had been the chief of the tribe.

But he heard nothing and said to himself, "They are all such fools that they don't know and don't care who murdered their chief!"

Little did he know in his so-called "monkey's wisdom" that this seeming unconcern was part of the young crab's plan. He purposely pretended not to know who killed his father, and also to believe that he had met his death through his own fault. By this means he could the better keep secret the revenge on the monkey, which he was meditating.

So the monkey returned home from his walk quite content. He told himself he had nothing now to fear.

One fine day, when the monkey was sitting at home, he was surprised by the appearance of a messenger from the young crab. While he was wondering what this might mean, the messenger bowed before him and said, "I have been sent by my master to inform you that his father died the other day in falling from a persimmon tree while trying to climb the tree after fruit. This, being the seventh day, is the first anniversary after his death, and my master has prepared a little festival in his father's honor, and bids you come to participate in it as you were one of his best friends. My master hopes you will honor his house with your kind visit."

When the monkey heard these words he rejoiced in his inmost heart, for all his fears of being suspected were now at rest. He could not guess that a plot had just been set in motion against him. He pretended to be very surprised at the news of the crab's death, and said: "I am, indeed, very sorry to hear of your chief's death. We were great friends as you know. I remember that we once exchanged a rice-dumpling for a persimmon-seed. It grieves me much to think that that seed was in the end the cause of his death. I accept your kind invitation with many thanks. I shall be delighted to do honor to my poor old friend!" And he screwed some false tears from his eyes.

The messenger laughed inwardly and thought, "The wicked monkey is now dropping false tears, but within a short time he shall shed real ones."

But aloud he thanked the monkey politely and went home.

When he had gone, the wicked monkey laughed aloud at what he thought was the young crab's innocence, and without the least feeling began to look forward to the feast to be held that day in honor of the dead crab, to which he had been invited. He changed his dress and set out solemnly to visit the young crab.

He found all the members of the crab's family and his relatives waiting to receive and welcome him. As soon as the bows of meeting were over they led him to a hall. Here the young chief mourner came to receive him. Expressions of condolence and thanks were exchanged between them, and then they all sat down to a luxurious feast and entertained the monkey as the guest of honor.

The feast over, he was next invited to the tea ceremony room to drink a cup of tea. When the young crab had conducted the monkey to the tearoom he left him and retired. Time passed and still he did not return. At last the monkey became impatient. He said to himself: "This tea ceremony is always a very slow affair. I am tired of waiting so long. I am very thirsty after drinking so much sake at the dinner!"

He then approached the charcoal fireplace and began to pour out some hot water from the kettle boiling there, when something burst out from the ashes with a great pop and hit the monkey right in the neck. It was the chestnut, one of the crab's friends, who had hidden himself in the fireplace. The monkey, taken by surprise, jumped backward, and then started to run out of the room.

The bee, who was hiding outside the screens, now flew out and stung him on the cheek. The monkey was in great pain, his neck was burned by the chestnut and his face badly stung by the bee, but he ran on screaming and chattering with rage.

Now the stone mortar had hidden himself with several other stones on the top of the crab's gate, and as the monkey ran underneath, the mortar and all fell down on the top of the monkey's head.

Was it possible for the monkey to bear the weight of the mortar falling on him from the top of the gate? He lay crushed and in great pain, quite unable to get up. As he lay there helpless the young crab came up, and, holding his great claw scissors over the monkey, he said: "Do you now remember that you murdered my father?"

"Then you are my enemy?" gasped the monkey brokenly.

"Of course," said the young crab.

"It was your father's fault not mine!" gasped the unrepentant monkey.

"Can you still lie? I will soon put an end to your breath!" and with that he cut off the monkey's head with his pincher claws. Thus the wicked monkey met his well-merited punishment, and the young crab avenged his father's death.

This is the end of the story of the monkey, the crab, and the persimmon-seed.

Source: "The Quarrel of the Monkey and the Crab," Yei Theodora Ozaki. *Japanese Fairy Tales.* (New York: Grosset and Dunlap, 1906), pp. 207–218.

The Story of the Old Man Who Made Withered Trees to Flower

As is the case in this tale, most Japanese American folktales end with the punishment of evil characters and rewards for the protagonists. The original Japanese version of the following tale, however, ends with an episode in which the greedy antagonists are given a share of the good old man's wealth. His generosity leads to the reform of the evil neighbor (compare this ending to "The Tongue-cut Sparrow" pp. 101–7). At some point, the second ending of the tale was lost, leaving the version recorded below.

Long, long ago there lived an old man and his wife who supported themselves by cultivating a small plot of land. Their life had been a very happy and peaceful one save for one great sorrow, and this was they had no child. Their only pet was a dog named Shiro, and on him they lavished all the affection of their old age. Indeed, they loved him so much that whenever they had anything nice to eat they denied themselves to give it to Shiro. Now Shiro means "white," and he was so called because of his color. He was a real Japanese dog, and very like a small wolf in appearance.

The happiest hour of the day both for the old man and his dog was when the man returned from his work in the field, and having finished his frugal supper of rice and vegetables, would take what he had saved from the meal out to the little veranda that ran round the cottage. Sure enough, Shiro was waiting for his master and an evening tidbit. Then the old man said "Chin, chin!" and Shiro sat up and begged, and his master gave him the food.

Next door to this good old couple there lived another old man and his wife who were both wicked and cruel, and who hated their good neighbors and the dog Shiro with all their might. Whenever Shiro happened to look into their kitchen they at once kicked him or threw something at him, sometimes even wounding him.

One day Shiro was heard barking for a long time in the field at the back of his master's house. The old man, thinking that perhaps some birds were attacking the corn, hurried out to see what was the matter. As soon as Shiro saw his master he ran to meet him, wagging his tail, and, seizing the end of his kimono, dragged him under a large yenoki tree. Here he began to dig very industriously with his paws, yelping with joy all the time. The old man, unable to understand what it all meant, stood looking on in bewilderment. But Shiro went on barking and digging with all his might.

He thought that something might be hidden beneath the tree, and that the dog had scented it, at last struck the old man. He ran back to the house, fetched his spade and began to dig the ground at that spot. What was his astonishment when, after digging for some time, he came upon a heap of old and valuable coins, and the deeper he dug the more gold coins did he find.

So intent was the old man on his work that he never saw the cross face of his neighbor peering at him through the bamboo hedge. At last all the gold coins lay shining on the ground. Shiro sat by erect with pride and looking fondly at his master as if to say, "You see, though only a dog, I can make some return for all the kindness you show me."

The old man ran in to call his wife, and together they carried home the treasure. Thus in one day the poor old man became rich. His gratitude to the faithful dog knew no bounds, and he loved and petted him more than ever, if that were possible.

The cross old neighbor, attracted by Shiro's barking, had been an unseen and envious witness of the finding of the treasure. He began to think that he, too, would like to find a fortune. So a few days later he called at the old man's house and very ceremoniously asked permission to borrow Shiro for a short time.

Shiro's master thought this a strange request, because he knew quite well that not only did his neighbor not love his pet dog, but that he never lost an opportunity of striking and tormenting him whenever the dog crossed his path. But the good old man was too kindhearted to refuse his neighbor, so he consented to lend the dog on condition that he should be taken great care of.

The wicked old man returned to his home with an evil smile on his face, and told his wife how he had succeeded in his crafty intentions. He then took his spade and hastened to his own field, forcing the unwilling Shiro to follow him. As soon as he reached a yenoki tree, he said to the dog, threateningly: "If there were gold coins under your master's tree, there must also be gold coins under my tree. You must find them for me! Where are they? Where? Where?"

And catching hold of Shiro's neck he held the dog's head to the ground, so that Shiro began to scratch and dig in order to free himself from the horrid old man's grasp.

The old man was very pleased when he saw the dog begin to scratch and dig, for he at once supposed that some gold coins lay buried under his tree as well as under his neighbor's, and that the dog had scented them as before; so pushing Shiro away he began to dig himself, but there was nothing to be found. As he went on digging a foul smell was noticeable, and he at last came upon a refuse heap.

The old man's disgust can be imagined. This soon gave way to anger. He had seen his neighbor's good fortune, and hoping for the same luck himself, he had borrowed the dog Shiro; and now, just as he seemed on the point of finding what he sought, only a horrid smelling refuse heap had rewarded him for a morning's digging. Instead of blaming his own greed for his disappointment, he blamed the poor dog. He seized his spade, and with all his strength struck Shiro and killed him on the spot. He then threw the dog's body into the hole which he had dug in the hope of finding a treasure of gold coins, and covered it over with the earth. Then he returned to the house, telling no one, not even his wife, what he had done.

After waiting several days, as the dog Shiro did not return, his master began to grow anxious. Day after day went by and the good old man waited in vain. Then he went to his neighbor and asked him to give him back his dog. Without any shame or hesitation, the wicked neighbor answered that he had killed Shiro because of his bad behavior. At this dreadful news Shiro's master wept many sad and bitter tears. Great indeed, was his woeful surprise, but he was too good and gentle to reproach his bad neighbor. Learning that Shiro was buried under the yenoki tree in the field, he asked the old man to give him the tree, in remembrance of his poor dog Shiro.

Even the cross old neighbor could not refuse such a simple request, so he consented to give the old man the tree under which Shiro lay buried. Shiro's master then cut the tree down and carried it home. Out of the trunk he made a mortar. In this his wife put some rice, and he began to pound it with the intention of making a festival to the memory of his dog Shiro.

A strange thing happened! His wife put the rice into the mortar, and no sooner had he begun to pound it to make the cakes, than it began to increase in quantity gradually till it was about five times the original amount, and the cakes were turned out of the mortar as if an invisible hand were at work.

When the old man and his wife saw this, they understood that it was a reward to them from Shiro for their faithful love to him. They tasted the cakes and found them nicer than any other food. So from this time they never troubled about food, for they lived upon the cakes with which the mortar never ceased to supply them.

The greedy neighbor, hearing of this new piece of good luck, was filled with envy as before, and called on the old man and asked leave to borrow the wonderful mortar for a short time, pretending that he, too, sorrowed for the death of Shiro, and wished to make cakes for a festival to the dog's memory.

The old man did not in the least wish to lend it to his cruel neighbor, but he was too kind to refuse. So the envious man carried home the mortar, but he never brought it back.

Several days passed, and Shiro's master waited in vain for the mortar, so he went to call on the borrower, and asked him to be good enough to return the mortar if he had finished with it. He found him sitting by a big fire made of pieces of wood. On the ground lay what looked very much like pieces of a broken mortar. In answer to the old man's inquiry, the wicked neighbor answered haughtily: "Have you come to ask me for your mortar? I broke it to pieces, and now I am making a fire of the wood, for when I tried to pound cakes in it only some horrid smelling stuff came out."

The good old man said: "I am very sorry for that. It is a great pity you did not ask me for the cakes if you wanted them. I would have given you as many as ever you wanted. Now please give me the ashes of the mortar, as I wish to keep them in remembrance of my dog."

The neighbor consented at once, and the old man carried home a basket full of ashes.

Not long after this the old man accidentally scattered some of the ashes made by the burning of the mortar on the trees of his garden. A wonderful thing happened!

It was late in autumn and all the trees had shed their leaves, but no sooner did the ashes touch their branches than the cherry trees, the plum trees, and all other blossoming shrubs burst into bloom, so that the old man's garden was suddenly transformed into a beautiful picture of spring. The old man's delight knew no bounds, and he carefully preserved the remaining ashes.

The story of the old man's garden spread far and wide, and people from far and near came to see the wonderful sight.

One day, soon after this, the old man heard some one knocking at his door, and going to the porch to see who it was he was surprised to see a Knight [samurai] standing there. This Knight told him that he was a retainer of a great Daimio [feudal lord]; that one of the favorite cherry trees in this nobleman's garden had withered, and that though everyone in his service had tried all manner of means to revive it, none took effect. The Knight was sore perplexed when he saw what great displeasure the loss of his favorite cherry tree caused the Daimio. At this point, fortunately, they had heard that there was a wonderful old man who could make withered trees to blossom, and that his Lord had sent him to ask the old man to come to him.

"And," added the Knight, "I shall be very much obliged if you will come at once."

The good old man was greatly surprised at what he heard, but respectfully followed the Knight to the nobleman's Palace.

The Daimio, who had been impatiently awaiting the old man's coming, as soon as he saw him asked him at once, "Are you the old man who can make withered trees flower even out of season?"

The old man made an obeisance, and replied: "I am that old man!"

Then the Daimio said, "You must make that dead cherry tree in my garden blossom again by means of your famous ashes. I shall look on."

Then they all went into the garden, the Daimio and his retainers and the ladies-in-waiting, who carried the Daimio's sword.

The old man now tucked up his kimono and made ready to climb the tree. Saying "Excuse me," he took the pot of ashes which he had brought with him, and began to climb the tree, every one watching his movements with great interest.

At last he climbed to the spot where the tree divided into two great branches, and taking up his position here, the old man sat down and scattered the ashes right and left all over the branches and twigs.

Wonderful, indeed, was the result! The withered tree at once burst into full bloom! The Daimio was so transported with joy that he looked as if he would go mad. He rose to his feet and spread out his fan, calling the old man down from the tree. He himself gave the old man a wine cup filled with the best sake, and rewarded him with much silver and gold and many other precious things. The Daimio ordered that henceforth the old man should call himself by the name of "Hana-Saka-Jijii," or "The Old Man who makes the Trees to Blossom," and that henceforth all were to recognize him by this name, and he sent him home with great honor.

The wicked neighbor, as before, heard of the good old man's fortune, and of all that had so auspiciously befallen him, and he could not suppress all the envy and jealousy that filled his heart. He called to mind how he had failed in his attempt to find the gold coins, and then in making the magic cakes; this time surely he must succeed if he imitated the old man, who made withered trees to flower simply by sprinkling ashes on them. This would be the simplest task of all.

So he set to work and gathered together all the ashes which remained in the fireplace from the burning of the wonderful mortar. Then he set out in the hope of finding some great man to employ him, calling out loudly as he went along, "Here comes the wonderful man who can make withered trees blossom! Here comes the old man who can make dead trees blossom!"

The Daimio in his Palace heard this cry, and said, "That must be the Hana-Saka-Jijii passing. I have nothing to do today. Let him try his art again; it will amuse me to look on."

So the retainers went out and brought in the impostor before their Lord. The satisfaction of the false old man can now be imagined.

But the Daimio looking at him, thought it strange that he was not at all like the old man he had seen before, so he asked him, "Are you the man whom I named Hana-Saka-Jijii?"

And the envious neighbor answered with a lie, "Yes, my Lord!"

"That is strange!" said the Daimio. "I thought there was only one Hana-Saka-Jijii in the world! Has he now some disciples?"

"I am the true Hana-Saka-Jijii. The one who came to you before was only my disciple!" replied the old man again.

"Then you must be more skillful than the other. Try what you can do and let me see!"

The envious neighbor, with the Daimio and his Court following, then went into the garden, and approaching a dead tree, took out a handful of the ashes which he carried with him, and scattered them over the tree.

But not only did the tree not burst into flower, but not even a bud came forth. Thinking that he had not used enough ashes, the old man took handfuls and again sprinkled them over the withered tree. But all to no effect. After trying several times, the ashes were blown into the Daimio's eyes.

This made him very angry, and he ordered his retainers to arrest the false Hana-Saka-Jijii at once and put him in prison for an impostor. From this imprisonment the wicked old man was never freed. Thus did he meet with punishment at last for all his evil doings.

The good old man, however, with the treasure of gold coins which Shiro had found for him, and with all the gold and the silver which the Daimio had showered on him, became a rich and prosperous man in his old age, and lived a long and happy life, beloved and respected by all.

Source: "The Old Man Who Made Withered Trees Flower," Yei Theodora Ozaki. *Japanese Fairy Tales.* (New York: Grosset and Dunlap, 1906), pp. 178–190.

The Magic Rice Kettle

The following narrative has been widely anthologized and retold in book form both in English and in Korean. The title commonly used in these reiterations is "The Magic Jewel" or "The Magic Gem," a reference to the gift of amber given to the protagonist in return for his generosity. The tale is often interpreted as an explanation for the enmity between dogs and cats. At least as important as the conflict between the old man's pets, however, is the message regarding loyalty and, by implication, the importance of maintaining family bonds during difficult times.

There was once an old man who was so poor he was scarcely able to buy food enough to keep him alive.

He had never married, and so he had no children, but he had a little dog and cat that lived with him, and these two he loved as though they were his own son and daughter. What little he had was shared with them, and if they were sometimes hungry, it was because he had nothing in the house to eat.

One day the old man found that all he had was one scant handful of rice.

"Alas, my little dog and cat, what will become of us now?" he cried. "This handful of rice is all that is left to keep us alive. After it is gone, you must seek another master who can feed you better than I. Even if I must starve, that is no reason why you should too."

The little cat mewed, and the dog looked up into his master's face, as though they had understood all he said to them.

The old man put the rice over the fire to cook, and just as it was done, and he was about to feed the animals, the light in the hut was darkened; looking round, he saw a tall stranger standing in the open doorway.

"Good day," said the stranger.

"Good day," answered the old man.

"I have come a long way," said the stranger, "and I am footsore and weary. May I come in and rest?"

Yes, he might do that and welcome.

The stranger came in and sat down in the most comfortable place. "I am hungry as well as weary."

"Alas," cried the old man, "this is a poor house in which to seek for food."

The stranger looked all about him. "Is not that rice that I see?" he asked, pointing to the kettle.

"Yes, it is rice, but my little dog and cat are hungry also, and not another morsel have we in the house beside that."

"Nevertheless, it is right that a man should be fed before dumb brutes," said the stranger. "Give me at least a taste of the rice before you feed them."

The old man did not know how to refuse him.

"Take some of it, then," he said, "but leave a little for them, I beg of you."

At once the stranger dipped into the kettle and began to eat, and he ate so fast that before the old man could stop him, all the rice was gone from the kettle, to the very last grain.

The old man was cut to the heart to think that his guest could have done this. Now his little dog and cat would have to go to bed hungry. All the same, he said nothing. He took up the empty kettle and was about to put it back on the shelf when the stranger said to him, "Fill the kettle with water and hang it over the fire again."

"Why should I do that?" asked the old man. "Water will not fill our stomachs or satisfy our hunger."

"Nevertheless, do as I bid you," said the stranger.

He spoke in such a way that the old man did not dare to disobey him. Muttering to himself, he filled the kettle with water and hung it over the fire.

The stranger drew out a piece of something that looked like amber and threw it in the pot. At once the water began to boil, and as it did so it became filled with rice. And such rice! The grains were twice as big as usual, and from them arose a smell more delicious than anything the old man had ever smelled before in all his life.

Filled with wonder and fear, he turned toward where the stranger had been sitting, but the guest was gone. He had disappeared, and only the little cat and dog were left in the room, waiting hungrily for their dinner.

The old man lifted the kettle from the fire and began to serve out the rice. And now a still more wonderful thing happened. No matter how much was dipped out from the kettle, still it was always full. He could hardly believe his eyes. He dipped and dipped. Soon all the pots and kettles and bowls in the house were full of rice, and still the more he took out the more there was.

"It is magic," cried the old man. "It must be that the amber the stranger threw in the pot was a charm. If so, puss and my dog and I need never suffer hunger again."

And so it turned out to be. As long as the amber was in the kettle, it was always full of rice to the brim. The rice was always fresh, and delicious too, so that not only the neighbours but the people from the village across the river came to buy it; and they paid well for it.

The little cat and dog grew fat and sleek. As for the man, he not only had enough to eat, but he was able to buy for himself all the clothes he needed and to make presents to those who were poorer than himself.

One evening the old man felt very tired. So many people had come through the day to buy rice that his arm quite ached with serving it out.

He took a bowl and filled it for the cat and dog, and was about to set it on the floor when he noticed to his surprise that the kettle was not as full as it had been. He took another bowl and dipped out some more of the rice. The kettle failed to fill itself.

Again he dipped, and the more he took out, the emptier the kettle grew. The old man was very much frightened. He plunged his hands into the rice that was left in the kettle and began to feel about for the charm, but it was not there. Somehow, that day, while he was dipping out the rice for his customers, he must have dipped out the charm, and some one had carried it off home with his bowl of rice.

The old man was ready to tear his hair with despair. At once he ran out and began to go about the neighborhood, knocking at all the doors and begging to know whether a piece of amber had been found in the rice the people there had bought that day. But every one told him no. They had found nothing in their bowls but rice.

Worn out with sorrow, he went back to his hut at last and threw himself on the floor to sleep. It was a long time, however, before he could close his eyes. Soon all the money that had been paid him for the rice would be spent, and he was too old to work. Then there would be nothing for him but the same poverty and hunger he had endured for so many years. And his little dog and cat would have to suffer with him unless they were wise enough to run away and seek another master. At last, toward morning, the old man fell asleep, and then the dog and cat began to talk together in low tones.

"This is a bad business," said the dog.

"Bad enough," answered puss. "Our master has been very careless. He deserves to suffer. As for me, I have no notion of being half-starved again the way I used to be. I shall go away and try to find another home where there will be more to eat than here."

"You are very ungrateful," answered the dog.

"Instead of planning to run away, you ought to set your wits to work to think how we can help our master."

"But how could we do that? I know of no way."

"Let us go out and hunt for the charm. Perhaps we can find it. Our sense of smell is so keen that if we came anywhere near where it is I am sure we could find it, however well it was hidden. We will go from house to house all through the village, if need be. I will nose about in the gardens and out-buildings, and you must manage to creep into the houses and hunt about through the rooms."

"Very well," answered the cat. "I am sure I would be glad enough to help our master, and to stay with him too, if only he could give us enough to eat."

So, early the next day, before the old man was awake, the dog and the cat started out together on their search. The people of the village were still asleep, but the cat managed to find a way to creep into several of the houses, and the dog searched about outside, as he had promised to do. But with all their searchings, they found nothing except some scraps of food here and there. These they ate, and so satisfied their hunger somewhat. Then, when night came, they returned home, footsore and weary.

The old man was very glad to see them. All day he had missed them and had wondered where they were. He had saved some supper for them and was surprised that they did not seem more hungry for it. He was still very sad.

All day people had been coming to the hut to buy rice from him, and when they found he had none to sell, they had been very much disappointed. Some of them had even been angry and had scolded him.

The following day the dog and cat continued their search, but night found them still unsuccessful. So it went on, day after day and week after week. At last they had visited every house in the village, but they had seen and heard nothing of the charm.

"Now you see how it is. We are only wasting our time," said the cat. "I knew we could not find it, and I, for one, shall begin to look for another home."

"Nay, but wait a bit," answered the dog. "Have you forgotten that many of our master's customers came from the village across the river? We have not searched there yet."

"No, nor will we as far as I am concerned," answered the cat. "I am no swimmer. I have no idea of getting drowned. If you want to search there, you will have to go by yourself."

The dog began to beg and plead with her. "Very soon," said he, "the river will be frozen, and then we can cross on the ice without your wetting even the smallest toe of your paw. Only come!"

"Very well," said the cat at last. "I will do it; but mind you, we must wait until the river is well frozen, and there is no chance of our breaking through."

The dog agreed to this, and so, one cold day, when the river was as hard as stone, the two friends crossed to the farther side, and at once began to search the houses there.

At the first house they found nothing. At the second it was the same thing; but no sooner had the cat entered the third house than she smelled something that reminded her of the rice that had bubbled up in the magic kettle. She made her way from one room to the other, and at last she came to a small upper chamber that seemed to be unused. And now she could smell the charm more strongly than ever, and the smell seemed to come from the top of a high chest of drawers.

With a bound puss leaped to the top of it and looked about her. There, pushed well back against the wall, was a heavy wooden box, and the moment the cat put her nose to the keyhole she knew that the charm was inside of it.

She had found the charm, and that was one thing, but how to get it out of the box was quite a different matter. The box was locked, and puss soon found it was impossible to raise the lid. She tried to push it off the chest of drawers, hoping that if it fell on the floor it might burst open, but the box was so heavy that she could not budge it a hair's breadth. It seemed a hopeless matter. If the dog were only there, no doubt he could have pushed the box off; but then he had no way of getting into the house and even if he did, he could not climb to the top of the chest of drawers.

But when puss went down to tell him about it, he did not seem to think it was such a hopeless matter after all. He was overjoyed that she had found the charm, and was sure that they could get it out of the box some way or other.

"What we need," said he, "is to get a good big rat to come and gnaw a hole in the box for us."

"Yes, but that is not so easy to do," said the cat. "The rats have no love for me, as you very well know. I have caught and eaten too many of them. I believe they would be glad to starve me to death if they only could."

"You might make a bargain with them," said the dog. "They would be glad enough to help you, if you, in return, would promise not to catch any of them for ten years to come."

Well, the cat did not want to make that bargain at all. She was too fond of catching the rats whenever she could. She and the dog argued about it for a long time, but at last she agreed to do as he wished.

The next thing was to get a message to the king of the rats, and puss knew of a way to manage that. She had seen a mouse-hole near one of the out-buildings, and now she set herself very patiently to wait beside it until the mouse should come out. She had to wait for a long time too.

Perhaps the mouse had heard the two friends prowling about. At any rate, it lay so still in its hole that no one would have guessed it was there at all except a cat. At length, toward evening, the mouse thought it might be safe to venture out. But scarcely had it poked its nose out of its hole when the cat pounced upon it and held it in her claws.

The mouse began to beg and plead for mercy. "Oh, good Mrs. Cat, oh, dear Mrs. Cat, spare me, I pray of you! I have a wife and five little mouselings at home, and they would surely die of grief if any harm came to me."

"I am not going to hurt you," answered the cat, though her mouth watered to eat it. "Instead, I am going to let you go, if you will promise to carry a message for me to the king of the rats."

When the mouse heard that the cat would let it go, it could hardly believe in its good fortune. It promised that it would do anything the cat wished it to, and at once the cat took her paws off it and set it free. Then she told it what the message was that she wished it to carry for her: she wished the king to send a rat to gnaw a hole in a box so that she could get a charm that was locked away in it; if the king would do this, she, in return, would promise not to hurt or harm any mouse or rat for ten long years.

The mouse listened attentively, and as soon as he was sure he quite understood the message he hurried away to carry it to the king of the rats.

He was only gone for a short time, and when he came back he brought a stout, strong young rat with him. This rat had been sent by the king, who was ready to agree to the bargain the cat had proposed, and had sent the strongest, sharpest-toothed rat he had to gnaw the hole in the box.

As soon as the cat heard this, she made her way back into the house, while the rat and the mouse followed close after her, leaving the dog to wait for them outside. The cat led the way to the upper room and showed the rat the box on the chest of drawers. At once he set to work on it. He gnawed and gnawed and gnawed, but the wood was as hard as stone, as well as very thick.

At last he gnawed through it, but the hole was too small for him to crawl through, and he was too exhausted to make it any larger. The cat, indeed, could reach her paw through, and could even feel the charm, but she could not hook it out, though she tried again and again. But here the mouse made itself of use. It slipped through the hole into the box and quickly brought the charm out in its mouth.

When the cat saw the charm she purred with joy. Once again she promised the rat and mouse that she would not even try to catch them or any of their kind for ten years. Then she took the charm in her mouth and ran down to where the dog was.

The dog was even more delighted than she when he saw the charm. "Oh, my dear master!" he cried. "How happy he will be."

"Yes," said the cat; "but now make haste. If the people in the house discover the charm is gone, they might suspect us, and follow us, and try to get it back."

"Come, then," said the dog. "But, oh, my dear master! I can hardly wait to show him the charm."

The cat and dog hurried on down to the river, but when they reached the bank they met with a new difficulty. The weather had suddenly turned very warm and the ice had begun to melt. In many places it was gone altogether, and where it was left it was too thin even to bear such small animals as themselves.

"And now what are we to do?" cried the cat. "We will never be able to get back to our village."

"Oh, yes, we can," replied the dog. "Do you mount upon my back. Dig your claws deep into my long hair and hold on tight, and I will carry you across."

The cat was terribly frightened at the thought of such a thing, but still she saw no other way to cross the river. She climbed upon the dog's back, fastened her claws well in his hair, and then he plunged into the water and began to swim across.

All went well until they neared the other bank. A crowd of children had gathered there to see the ice break up. When they saw the dog swimming across with the cat on his back, it seemed to them the funniest thing they had ever seen in all their lives.

The dog was so busy swimming that he did not even notice them, but the cat, upon his back, saw everything that was going on. She herself suddenly began to think what a funny thing it was that she should be riding at ease on the dog's back, while he was swimming so hard.

She tried not to laugh, but she was so amused that at last she could refrain no longer. She burst into a loud cat-laugh, and at once the charm slipped from her mouth plump into the river, and sank to the bottom.

"The charm! The charm!" the cat cried. "I have dropped it in the river, and it has sunk to the bottom."

As soon as the dog heard that, he dived down into the river to regain it. He was in such a hurry that he never thought of telling the cat of what he meant to do.

The cat's claws were fastened so firmly in his hair that she could not have let go if she had wished. Also her mouth was open, so that when they went down into the river she swallowed a great deal of water. By the time the dog came to the top again, panting and snorting, the cat was almost drowned.

But the dog was too angry to think anything of that. "Wait till we get to the shore," he growled. "Just wait until we get to the shore, and see what I will do to you for dropping the charm."

But the cat had no idea of waiting for this. As they came near the shore, she bounded from the dog's back to the dry land, and then she raced away and up a tall tree.

The dog chased after her, but he could not catch her. For some time he stood at the foot of the tree, barking and growling, but at last he trotted on home with drooping head and ears and a sad heart. The old man was very glad to welcome the dog home again. He had feared it was lost. He looked out from the door in all directions, hoping to see the cat also, but the cat, which had now climbed down from the tree, had gone to look for another home. It feared the dog's anger too much to venture back to the hut. Moreover, it had no liking for poverty and hunger, and it hoped to find some place where it would be better fed than with the old man.

And now indeed there were hard times in the hut. The old man grew poorer and poorer, and thinner and thinner, and it was just as bad with the faithful dog. The dog spent much of his time down at the river looking sadly at the place where the charm had been lost and wishing there were some way for him to find it.

Now there was a great deal of fishing done in that river, and sometimes one of the fishermen, more kindhearted than the rest, would throw a fish to the hungry dog. This the dog always carried home to his master, and the two faithful friends would share it together. It was always a feast day when this happened.

One day one of the fishermen, who had been very lucky, called to the dog and threw him a particularly large fish. The dog caught it in his mouth and started home with it. Suddenly he smelled something: it was like the magic rice that had bubbled up in the pot; it must be the charm; it could be nothing but that; and the smell came from the fish he was carrying in his mouth. As soon as the dog was sure of this, he began to run. He could not get home fast enough. He reached the hut and bounded in and laid the fish upon the table.

"Good dog! Good dog!" cried his master. "Have you brought us a fine dinner today?" He took his knife and began to prepare the fish, but scarcely had he cut into it before the blade struck against something hard. The old man looked to see what it was, and what was his joy and amazement to find that it was the charm, which the fish must have swallowed. The old man was so delighted that he hardly knew how to contain himself.

"Oh, my precious charm!" he cried. "Oh, what good fortune! Oh, how happy I am! Wait until I fill the kettle, my dear little dog, and then what a feast we will have."

He took out the pot and filled it with water, and hung it over the fire. Then he threw the charm into it. At once the rice began to boil and bubble up. The whole house was filled with the delicious smell of it.

It did not take long for the neighbors to find out that the old man had his wonderful rice again. They hastened to buy of him, and soon he had made even more money than before.

One day the cat, which had grown very lean and thin, came sneaking into the house with one of the customers. As soon as the dog saw her he gave a snarl and was about to fly at her, but the old man caught the cat up in his arms. "Oh, my dear little cat," he cried, "how glad I am to see you. But how thin you have grown! Never mind; there is plenty in the house now, and soon you will grow fat again."

So the cat came back to her master again, but for as long as she lived the dog never forgave her, and they never became friends again. The old man did not know that however. He loved them both; he was quite happy to have them as companions, and lived very prosperous and contented until the end of his days.

Source: "The Magic Rice Kettle," Katharine Pyle. *Wonder Tales from Many Lands.* (London: George G. Harrap and Company, Ltd., 1910), pp. 160–176.

The Story of Chang To-Ryong

The following legend, although set in Korea and based in Chinese Taoist supernatural beliefs, has continuing relevance in contemporary society. As in many of the Asian texts contained in this collection, humble appearances often conceal extraordinary powers, and charity to the powerless is inevitably rewarded.

In the days of King Chung-jong (A.D. 1507–1526) there lived a beggar in Seoul, whose face was extremely ugly and always dirty. He was forty years of age or so, but still wore his hair down his back like an unmarried boy. He carried a bag over his shoulder, and went about the streets begging. During the day he went from one part of the city to the other, visiting each section, and when night came on he would huddle up beside someone's gate and go to sleep. He was frequently seen in Chong-no (Bell Street) in company with the servants and underlings of the rich.

They were great friends, he and they, joking and bantering as they met. He used to say that his name was Chang, and so they called him Chang To-ryong, To-ryong meaning an unmarried boy, son of the gentry. At that time the magician Chon U-chi, who was far-famed for his pride and arrogance, whenever he met Chang, in passing along the street, would dismount and prostrate himself most humbly. Not only did he bow, but he seemed to regard Chang with the greatest of fear, so that he dared not look him in the face. Chang, sometimes, without even inclining his head, would say, "Well, how goes it with you, eh?"

Chon, with his hands in his sleeves, most respectfully would reply, "Very well, sir, thank you, very well." He had fear written on all his features when he faced Chang.

Sometimes, too, when Chon would bow, Chang would refuse to notice him at all, and go by without a word. Those who saw it were astonished, and asked Chon the reason. Chon said in reply, "There are only three spirit-men at present in Cho-sen, of whom the greatest is Chang To-ryong; the second is Cheung Puk-chang; and the third is Yun Se-pyong. People of the world do not know it, but I do. Such being the case, should I not bow before him and show him reverence?"

Those who heard this explanation, knowing that Chon himself was a strange being, paid no attention to it.

At that time in Seoul there was a certain literary undergraduate in office whose house joined hard on the street. This man used to see Chang frequently going about begging, and one day he called him and asked who he was, and why he begged. Chang made answer, "I was originally of a cultured family of Chulla Province, but my parents died of typhus fever, and I had no brothers or relations left to share my lot. I alone remained of all my clan, and having no home of my own I have gone about begging, and have at last reached Seoul. As I am not skilled in any handicraft, and do not know Chinese letters, what else can I do?"

The undergraduate, hearing that he was a scholar, felt very sorry for him, gave him food and drink, and refreshed him. From this time on, whenever there was any special celebration at his home, he used to call Chang in and have him share it.

On a certain day when the master was on his way to office, he saw a dead body being carried on a stretcher off toward the Water Gate. Looking at it closely from the horse on which he rode, he recognized it as the corpse of Chang To-ryong. He felt so sad that he turned back to his house and cried over it, saying, "There are lots of miserable people on earth, but who ever saw one as miserable as poor Chang? As I reckon the time over on my fingers, he has been begging in Bell Street for fifteen years, and now he passes out of the city a dead body."

Twenty years and more afterwards the master had to make a journey through South Chulla Province. As he was passing Chi-i Mountain, he lost his way and got into a maze among the hills. The day began to wane, and he could neither return nor go forward. He saw a narrow footpath, such as woodmen take, and turned into it to see if it led to any habitation. As he went along there were rocks and deep ravines. Little by little, as he advanced farther, the scene changed and seemed to become strangely transfigured. The farther he went the more wonderful it became.

After he had gone some miles he discovered himself to be in another world entirely, no longer a world of earth and dust. He saw some one coming toward him dressed in ethereal green, mounted and carrying a shade, with servants accompanying. He seemed to sweep toward him with swiftness and without effort. He thought to himself, "Here is some high lord or other coming to meet me, but," he added, "how among these deeps and solitudes could a gentleman come riding so?"

He led his horse aside and tried to withdraw into one of the groves by the side of the way, but before he could think to turn the man had reached him. The mysterious stranger lifted his two hands in salutation and inquired respectfully as to how he had been all this time. The master was speechless, and so astonished that he could make no reply. But the stranger smilingly said, "My house is quite near here; come with me and rest." He turned, and leading the way seemed to glide and not to walk, while the master followed. At last they reached the place indicated. He suddenly saw before him great palace halls filling whole squares of space. Beautiful buildings they were, richly ornamented. Before the door attendants in official robes awaited them. They bowed to the master and led him into the hall.

After passing a number of gorgeous, palace-like rooms, he arrived at a special one and ascended to the upper storey, where he met a very wonderful person. He was dressed in shining garments, and the servants that waited on him were exceedingly fair. There were, too, children about, so exquisitely beautiful that it seemed none other than a celestial palace. The master, alarmed at finding himself in such a place, hurried forward and made a low obeisance, not daring to lift his eyes. But the host smiled upon him, raised his hands and asked, "Do you not know me? Look now."

Lifting his eyes, he then saw that it was the same person who had come riding out to meet him, but he could not tell who he was. "I see you," said he, "but as to who you are I cannot tell."

The kingly host then said, "I am Chang To-ryong. Do you not know me?" Then as the master looked more closely at him he could see the same features. The outlines of the face were there, but all the imperfections had gone, and only beauty remained. So wonderful was it that he was quite overcome.

A great feast was prepared, and the honored guest was entertained. Such food, too, was placed before him as was never seen on earth. Angelic beings played on beautiful instruments and danced as no mortal eye ever looked upon. Their faces, too, were like pearls and precious stones.

Chang To-ryong said to his guest, "There are four famous mountains in Korea in which the genii reside. This hill is one. In days gone by, for a fault of mine, I was exiled to earth, and in the time of my exile you treated me with marked kindness, a favor that I have never forgotten. When you saw my dead body your pity went out to me; this, too, I remember. I was not dead then, it was simply that my days of exile were ended and I was returning home. I knew that you were passing this hill, and I desired to meet you and to thank you for all your kindness. Your treatment of me in another world is sufficient to bring about our meeting in this one." And so they met and feasted in joy and great delight.

When night came he was escorted to a special pavilion, where he was to sleep. The windows were made of jade and precious stones, and soft lights came streaming through them, so that there was no night. "My body was so rested and my soul so refreshed," said he, "that I felt no need of sleep."

When the day dawned a new feast was spread, and then farewells were spoken. Chang said, "This is not a place for you to stay long in; you must go. The ways differ of we genii and you men of the world. It will be difficult for us ever to meet again. Take good care of yourself and go in peace." He then called a servant to accompany him and show the way. The master made a low bow and withdrew. When he had gone but a short distance he suddenly found himself in the old world with its dusty accompaniments. The path by which he came out was not the way by which he had entered. In order to mark the entrance he planted a stake, and then the servant withdrew and disappeared.

The year following the master went again and tried to find the citadel of the genii, but there were only mountain peaks and impassable ravines, and where it was he never could discover.

As the years went by the master seemed to grow younger in spirit, and at last at the age of ninety he passed away without suffering. "When Chang was here on earth and I saw him for fifteen years," said the master, "I remember but one peculiarity about him, namely, that his face never grew older nor did his dirty clothing ever wear out. He never changed his garb, and yet it never varied in appearance in all the fifteen years. This alone would have marked him as a strange being, but our fleshly eyes did not recognize it."

Source: "The Story of ChangTo-Ryong," James S. Gale. *Korean Folktales: Imps, Ghosts, and Fairies.* (New York: E.P. Dutton & Co., 1913), pp. 17–25.

THE SUPERNATURAL

An Encounter with a Hobgoblin

The supernatural beings described in the following tale are to-kkae-bi. These entities may be either benevolent or malicious, mischievous or ominous. They also are said to possess great physical strength. Although their usual form is anthropomorphic, they have the ability to shape-shift into virtually any form they wish. The editor of this tale notes, "If a good or 'superior man' enters such a place [a haunted dwelling] the goblins move away." The fact that the to-kkae-bi were not driven away by Choi but instead they injured him offers evidence of his poor character—as does his imprisonment. Therefore, Choi represents a model for avoidance in traditional Korean culture.

I got myself into trouble in the year Pyong-sin, and was locked up; a military man by the name of Choi Won-so, who was captain of the guard, was involved in it and locked up as well. We often met in prison and whiled away the hours talking together. On a certain day the talk turned on goblins, when Captain Choi said, "When I was young I met with a hobgoblin, which, by the fraction of a hair, almost cost me my life. A strange case indeed!"

I asked him to tell me of it, when he replied, "I had originally no home in Seoul, but hearing of a vacant place, I made application and got it. We went there, my father and the rest of the family occupying the inner quarters, while I lived in the front room.

"One night, late, when I was half asleep, the door suddenly opened, and a woman came in and stood just before the lamp. I saw her clearly, and knew that she was from the home of a scholar friend, for I had seen her before and had been greatly attracted by her beauty, but had never had a chance to meet her. Now, seeing her enter the room thus, I greeted her gladly, but she made no reply. I arose to take her by the hand, when she began walking backwards, so that my hand never reached her. I rushed towards her, but she hastened her backward pace, so that she eluded me. We reached the gate, which she opened with a rear kick, and I followed on after, till she suddenly disappeared. I searched on all sides, but not a trace was there of her. I thought she had merely hidden herself, and never dreamed of anything else.

"On the next night she came again and stood before the lamp just as she had done the night previous. I got up and again tried to take hold of her, but again she began her peculiar pace backwards, till she passed out at the gate and disappeared just as she had done the day before. I was once more surprised and disappointed, but did not think of her being a hobgoblin.

"A few days later, at night, I had lain down, when suddenly there was a sound of crackling paper overhead from above the ceiling. A forbidding, creepy sound it seemed in the midnight.

"A moment later a curtain was let down that divided the room into two parts. Again, later, a large fire of coals descended right in front of me, while an immense heat filled the place. Where I was seemed all on fire, with no way of escape possible. In terror for my life, I knew not what to do. On the first cock-crow of morning the noise ceased, the curtain went up, and the fire of coals was gone. The place was as though swept with a broom, so clean from every trace of what had happened.

"The following night I was again alone, but had not yet undressed or lain down, when a great stout man suddenly opened the door and came in. He had on his head a soldier's felt hat, and on his body a blue tunic like one of the underlings of the yamen. He took hold of me and tried to drag me out. I was then young and vigorous, and had no intention of yielding to him, so we entered on a tussle. The moon was bright and the night clear, but I, unable to hold my own, was pulled out into the court. He lifted me up and swung me round and round, then went up to the highest terrace and threw me down, so that I was terribly stunned. He stood in front of me and kept me a prisoner. There was a garden to the rear of the house, and a wall round it. I looked, and within the wall were a dozen or so of people. They were all dressed in military hats and coats, and they kept shouting out, 'Don't hurt him, don't hurt him.'

"The man that mishandled me, however, said in reply, 'It's none of your business, none of your business'; but they still kept up the cry, 'Don't hurt him, don't hurt him'; and he, on the other hand, cried, 'Never you mind; none of your business.' They shouted, 'The man is a gentleman of the military class; do not hurt him.'

"The fellow merely said in reply, 'Even though he is, it's none of your business'; so he took me by the two hands and flung me up into the air, till I went half-way and more to heaven. Then in my fall I went shooting past Kyong-keui Province, past Choong-chong, and at last fell to the ground in Chulla. In my flight through space I saw all the county towns of the three provinces as clear as day. Again in Chulla he tossed me up once more. Again I went shooting up into the sky and falling north-ward, till I found myself at home, lying stupefied below the verandah terrace. Once more I could hear the voices of the group in the garden shouting, 'Don't hurt him.' But the man said, 'None of your business.'

"He took me up once more and flung me up again, and away I went speeding off to Chulla, and back I came again, two or three times in all.

"Then one of the group in the garden came forward, took my tormentor by the hand and led him away. They all met for a little to talk and laugh over the matter, and then scattered and were gone, so that they were not seen again.

"I lay motionless at the foot of the terrace till the following morning, when my father found me and had me taken in hand and cared for, so that I came to, and we all left the haunted house, never to go back."

Source: "An Encounter with a Hobgoblin," James S. Gale. *Korean Folktales: Imps, Ghosts, and Fairies.* (New York: E.P. Dutton & Co., 1913), pp. 141–145.

Evil Eye of Sani

The following Hindu tale may be read as an allegory. Sani as a deity is associated with misfortune and destruction. In Hindu astrology, Sani is the inauspicious planet Saturn. In contrast, Lakshmi is the goddess of domestic harmony, wealth, and prosperity. Sribatsa is literally translated as the "child of fortune." Caught in a contest between Sani and Lakshmi, Sribatsa is a Hindu "Everyman," who is tossed about at the whim of good and evil fortune. A reflection of the universal human condition, the narrative is appropriate to both Asian and Asian American contexts.

Once upon a time Sani, the god of bad luck, and Lakshmi, the goddess of good luck, fell out with each other in heaven. Sani said he was higher in rank than Lakshmi, and Lakshmi said she was higher in rank than Sani. As all the gods and goddesses of heaven were equally ranged on either side, the contending deities agreed to refer the matter to some human being who had a name for wisdom and justice. Now, there lived at that time upon earth a man of the name of Sribatsa, who was as wise and just as he was rich. He, therefore, both the god and the goddess chose as the settler of their dispute.

One day, accordingly, Sribatsa was told that Sani and Lakshmi were wishing to pay him a visit to get their dispute settled. Sribatsa was in a fix. If he said Sani was higher in rank than Lakshmi, she would be angry with him and forsake him. If he said Lakshmi was higher in rank than Sani, Sani would cast his evil eye upon him. Hence he made up his mind not to say anything directly, but to leave the god and the goddess to gather his opinion from his action, He got two stools made, the one of gold and the other of silver, and placed them beside him.

When Sani and Lakshmi came to Sribatsa, he told Sani to sit upon the silver stool, and Lakshmi upon the gold stool. Sani became mad with rage, and said in an angry tone to Sribatsa, "Well, as you consider me lower in rank than Lakshmi, I will cast my eye on you for three years; and I should like to see how you fare at the end of that period."

The god then went away in high dudgeon, Lakshmi, before going away, said to Sribatsa, "My child, do not fear. I'll befriend you."

The god and the goddess then went away. Sribatsa said to his wife, whose name was Chintamani, "Dearest, as the evil eye of Sani will be upon me at once, I had better go away from the house; for if I remain in the house with you, evil will befall you and me, but if I go away, it will overtake me only."

Chintamani said, "That I cannot do; wherever you go, I will go, your lot shall be my lot. The husband tried hard to persuade his wife to remain at home, but it was of no use. She would go with her husband.

Sribatsa accordingly told his wife to make an opening in their mattress, and to stow away in it all the money and jewels they had. On the eve of leaving their house, Sribatsa invoked Lakshmi, who forthwith, appeared. He then said to her, "Mother Lakshmi, as the evil eye of Sani is upon us, we are going away into exile; but do thou befriend us, and take care of our house and property."

The goddess of good luck answered, "Do not fear; I'll befriend you; all will be right at last.

They then set out on their journey. Sribatsa rolled up the mattress and put it on his head. They had not gone many miles when they saw a river before them. It was not fordable; but there was a canoe there with a man sitting in it. The travelers requested the ferryman to take them across.

The ferryman said, "I can take only one at a time; but you are three, yourself, your wife, and the mattress."

Sribatsa proposed that first his wife and the mattress should be taken across, and then he; but the ferryman would not hear of it. "Only one at a time," repeated he; " first let me take across the mattress." When the canoe with the mattress was in the middle of the stream, a fierce gale arose, and carried away the mattress, the canoe, and the ferryman, no one knows whither. And it was strange the stream also disappeared, for the place, where they saw a few minutes since the rush of waters, had now become firm ground.

Sribatsa then knew that this was nothing but the evil eye of Sani.

Sribatsa and his wife, without a coin in their pocket, went to a village which was hard by. It was dwelt in for the most part by wood-cutters, who used to go at sunrise to the forest to cut wood, which they sold in a town not far from the village. Sribatsa proposed to the wood-cutters that he should go along with them to cut wood. They agreed. So he began to fell trees as well as the best of them; but there was this difference between Sribatsa and the other wood-cutters, that whereas the latter cut any and every sort of wood, the former cut only precious wood like sandal-wood. The wood-cutters used to bring to market large loads of common wood, and Sribatsa only a few pieces of sandal-wood, for which he got a great deal more money than the others. As this was going on day after day, the wood-cutters through envy plotted together, and drove away from the village Sribatsa and his wife.

The next place they went to was a village of weavers or rather cotton-spinners. Here Chintamani, the wife of Sribatsa, made herself useful by spinning cotton. As she was an intelligent and skilful woman, she spun finer thread than the other women; and she got more money. This roused the envy of the native women of the village. But this was not all. Sribatsa in order to gain the good grace of the weavers asked them to a feast, the dishes of which were all cooked by his wife. As Chintamani excelled in cooking, the barbarous weavers of the village were quite charmed by the delicacies set before them. When the men went to their homes, they reproached their wives for not being able to cook so well as the wife of Sribatsa, and called them good-for-nothing women. This thing made the women of the village hate Chintamani the more.

One day Chintamani went to the river side to bathe along with the other women of the village. A boat had been lying on the bank stranded on the sand for many days; they had tried to move it, but in vain. It so happened that as Chintamani by accident touched the boat, it moved off to the river. The boatmen, astonished at the event, thought that the woman had uncommon power, and might be useful on similar occasions in future. They therefore caught hold of her, put her in the boat and rowed off. The women of the village, who were present, did not offer any resistance as they hated Chintamani. When Sribatsa heard how his wife had been carried away by boatmen, he became mad with grief. He left the village, went to the riverside and resolved to follow the course of the stream till he should meet the boat where his wife was a prisoner. He travelled on and on, along the side of the river till it became dark. As there were no huts to be seen, he climbed into a tree for the night. Next morning as he got down from the tree he saw at the foot of it a cow called a Kapila-cow, which never calves, but which gives milk at all hours of the day whenever it is milked. Sribatsa milked the cow, and drank its milk to his heart's content. He was astonished to find that the cow-dung which lay on the ground was of a bright yellow color; indeed, he found it was pure gold.

While it was in a soft state he wrote his own name upon it, and when in the course of the day it became hardened, it looked like a brick of gold and so it was. As the tree grew on the river side, and as the Kapila-cow came morning and evening to supply him with milk, Sribatsa resolved to stay there till he should meet the boat. In the meantime the gold-bricks were increasing in number every day, for the cow both morning and evening deposited there the precious article. He put the gold-bricks, upon all of which his name was engraved, one upon another in rows, so that from a distance they looked like a hillock of gold.

Leaving Sribatsa to arrange his gold-bricks under the tree on the river side we must follow the fortunes of his wife. Chintamani was a woman of great beauty; and thinking that her beauty might be her ruin, she, when seized by the boatmen, offered to Lakshmi the following prayer "Mother Lakshmi!

Have pity upon me. Thou hast made me beautiful, but now my beauty will undoubtedly prove my ruin by the loss of honor and chastity. I therefore beseech thee, gracious Mother, to make me ugly, and to cover my body with some loathsome disease, that the boatmen may not touch me." Lakshmi heard Chintamani's prayer, and in the twinkling of an eye, while she was in the arms of the boatmen, her naturally beautiful form was turned into a vile carcass. The boatmen on putting her down in the boat, found her body covered with loathsome sores which were giving out a disgusting stench. They therefore threw her into the hold of the boat amongst the cargo, where they used morning and evening to send her a little boiled rice and some water.

In that hold Chintamani had a miserable life of it; but she greatly preferred that misery to the loss of chastity. The boatmen went to some port, sold the cargo, and were returning to their country when the sight of what seemed a hillock of gold, not far from the river side, attracted their attention. Sribatsa, whose eyes were ever directed towards the river, was delighted when he saw a boat turn towards the bank, as he fondly imagined his wife might be in it. The boatmen went to the hillock of gold, when Sribatsa said that the gold was his. They put all the gold bricks on board their vessel, took Sribatsa prisoner, and put him into the hold not far from the woman covered with sores.

They of course immediately recognized each other, in spite of the change Chintamani had undergone, but thought it prudent not to speak to each other. They communicated their ideas therefore by signs and gestures. Now, the boatmen were fond of playing at dice, and as Sribatsa appeared to them from his looks to be a respectable man, they always asked him to join in the game. As he was an expert player, he almost always won the game, on which the boatmen, envying his superior skill, threw him overboard.

Chintamani had the presence of mind, at that moment, to throw into the water a pillow which she had for resting her head upon. Sribatsa took hold of the pillow, by means of which he floated down the stream till he was carried at nightfall to what seemed a garden on the water's edge. There he stuck among the trees, where he remained the whole night, wet and shivering.

Now, the garden belonged to an old widow who was in former years the chief flower-supplier to the king of that country. Through some cause or other a blight seemed to have come over her garden, as almost all the trees and plants ceased flowering; she had therefore given up her place as the flower-supplier of the royal household. On the morning following the night on which Sribatsa had stuck among the trees, however, the old woman on getting up from her bed could scarcely believe her eyes when she saw the whole garden ablaze with flowers. There was not a single tree or plant which was not begemmed with flowers.

Not understanding the cause of such a miraculous sight, she took a walk through the garden, and found on the river's brink, stuck among the trees, a man shivering and almost dying with cold. She brought him to her cottage, lighted a fire to give him warmth, and showed him every attention, as she ascribed the wonderful flowering of her trees to his presence. After making him as comfortable as she could, she ran to the king's palace, and told his chief servants that she was again in a position to supply the palace with flowers; so she was restored to her former office as the flower-woman of the royal household.

Sribatsa, who stopped a few days with the woman, requested her to recommend him to one of the king's ministers for a berth. He was accordingly sent for to the palace, and as he was at once found to be a man of intelligence, the king's minister asked him what post he would like to have.

In keeping with his wish he was appointed collector of tolls on the river. While discharging his duties as river toll-gatherer, in the course of a few days he saw the very boat in which his wife was a prisoner. He detained the boat, and charged the boatmen with the theft of gold-bricks which he claimed as his own. At the mention of gold-bricks the king himself came to the river side, and was astonished beyond measure to see bricks made of gold, every one of which had the inscription SRIBATSA. At the same time Sribatsa rescued from the boatmen his wife, who, the moment she came out of the vessel, became as lovely as before. The king heard the story of Sribatsa's misfortunes from his lips, entertained him in a princely style for many days, and at last sent him and his wife to their own country with presents of horses and elephants.

The evil eye of Sani was now turned away from Sribatsa, and he again became what he formerly was, the Child of Fortune.

Thus my story endeth.

Source: "The Evil Eye of Sani," Lal Behari Day. *Folk-Tales of Bengal.* (New York: The MacMillan Company, 1902), pp. 108–116.

The Fearless Captain

The behavior of the protagonist in this narrative, Yee Man-ji, should be contrasted to the behavior and character of Choi Won-so, the protagonist of "An Encounter with a Hobgoblin" (pp. 135–37). Traditional Korean beliefs hold that fear and weak character encourage supernatural attacks.

Men have been killed by goblins. This is not so much due to the fact that goblins are wicked as to the fact that men are afraid of them. Many died in North Ham-kyong, but those again who were brave, and clove them with a knife, or struck them down, lived. If they had been afraid, they too would have died.

There was formerly a soldier, Yee Man-ji of Yong-nam, a strong and muscular fellow, and brave as a lion. He had green eyes and a terrible countenance. Frequently he said, "Fear! What is fear?"

On a certain day when he was in his house a sudden storm of rain came on, when there were flashes of lightning and heavy claps of thunder. At one of them a great ball of fire came tumbling into his home and went rolling over the verandah, through the rooms, into the kitchen and out into the yard, and again into the servants' quarters.

Several times it went and came bouncing about. Its blazing light and the accompanying noise made it a thing of terror.

Yee sat in the outer verandah, wholly undisturbed. He thought to himself, "I have done no wrong, therefore why need I fear the lightning?"

A moment later a flash struck the large elm tree in front of the house and smashed it to pieces. The rain then ceased and the thunder likewise.

Yee turned to see how it fared with his family, and found them all fallen senseless. With the greatest of difficulty he had them restored to life.

During that year they all fell ill and died, and Yee came to Seoul and became a Captain of the Right Guard. Shortly after he went to North Ham-kyong Province. There he took a second wife and settled down. All his predecessors had died of goblin influences, and the fact that calamity had overtaken them while in the official quarters had caused them to use one of the village houses instead. Yee, however, determined to live down all fear and go back to the old quarters, which he extensively repaired.

One night his wife was in the inner room while he was alone in the public office with a light burning before him. In the second watch or thereabout, a strange-looking object came out of the inner quarters. It looked like the stump of a tree wrapped in black sackcloth. There was no outline or definite shape to it, and it came jumping along and sat itself immediately before Yee Man-ji. Also two other objects came following in its wake, shaped just like the first one. The three then sat in a row before Yee, coming little by little closer and closer to him. Yee moved away till he had backed up against the wall and could go no farther. Then he said, "Who are you, anyhow; what kind of devil, pray, that you dare to push towards me so in my office? If you have any complaint or matter to set right, say so, and I'll see to it."

The middle devil said in reply, "I'm hungry, I'm hungry, I'm hungry."

Yee answered, "Hungry, are you? Very well, now just move back and I'll have food prepared for you in abundance." He then repeated a magic formula that he had learned, and snapped his fingers. The three devils seemed to be afraid of this.

Then Man-ji suddenly closed his fist and struck a blow at the first devil. It dodged, however, most deftly and he missed, but hit the floor a sounding blow that cut his hand.

Then they all shouted, "We'll go, we'll go, since you treat guests thus." At once they bundled out of the room and disappeared.

On the following day he had oxen killed and a sacrifice offered to these devils, and they returned no more.

Source: "The Fearless Captain," James S. Gale. *Korean Folktales: Imps, Ghosts, and Fairies.* (New York: E.P. Dutton & Co., 1913), pp. 162–164.

The Anting-Anting of Manuelito

Despite the contrast of the anting-anting to the Christian scapular mentioned below, it is not uncommon to incorporate Christian symbols and phrases into these protective amulets. In the United States, knowledge and at times the utilization of the anting-anting have been perpetuated among practitioners of Filipino martial arts such as arnis or eskrima (stick fighting). Legends of bandit heroes having supernatural protection are common, especially during periods of political conflict when the bandit is seen as a representative of a relatively powerless group attempting to survive political or economic domination.

The Anting-Anting is a stone or other small object covered with cabalistic inscriptions. It is worn around the neck, and is supposed to render its owner impervious to knife or bullet. Many are wearing these charms, especially the *Tulisanes,* or outlaws. The Anting-Anting must not be confused, however, with the scapular, a purely religious symbol worn by a great number of the Christian Filipinos.

Many of the older Filipinos remember Manuelito, the great Tulisane [*sic* tulisan], who, more than fifty years ago, kept all the Laguna de Bai district in a state of fear. His robber band was well organized and obeyed his slightest wish. He had many boats on the lake and many hiding places in the mountains, and throughout the country there was no villager who did not fear to oppose him, or who would refuse to help him in any way when required to do so.

In vain the Guardia Civil [Civil Guard, military police force operating during the final decades of the Spanish Period] hunted him. Many times they surrounded the band, but Manuelito always escaped. Many shots were fired at him, but he was never hit; and once, when he was cut off from his men and surrounded, he broke through the line, and though fifty bullets whistled around him he did not receive a scratch.

The officers of the Guardia Civil blamed their men for the bad marksmanship that allowed Manuelito to escape. They told all the people that it should never occur again, and promised that the next fight should end in the death of the outlaw. The people, however, did not believe that

Manuelito could be killed, for he wore on his breast a famous Anting-Anting that he had received from Mangagauay, the giver of life and death.

This charm was a stone covered with mysterious signs. It was wrapped in silk and hung by a string from the robber's neck, and even if a gun were fired within a few feet of him the Anting-Anting was sure to turn the bullet in another direction. It was this charm that always saved him from the Guardia Civil.

Manuelito was very proud of his Anting-Anting, and many times, when a fiesta was being held in some town, he and his band would come down from the mountains and take part in the games. Manuelito would stand in the town plaza and allow his men to shoot at him, and each time the Anting-Anting would turn aside the bullets. The people were very much impressed, and though a few of the wiser ones secretly thought that the guns were only loaded with powder, they were afraid to say anything; so the greater number thought it very wonderful and believed that there was no charm so powerful as the Anting-Anting of Manuelito.

For years the Tulisane, protected by his charm, continued to rob and plunder. The Guardia Civil hunted him everywhere, but could never kill him. He grew bolder and bolder, and even came close to Manila to rob the little towns just outside the city.

At last the government grew tired of sending out the Guardia Civil, and ordered a regiment of Macabebes [Filipino nationals who served as mercenaries and scouts for the Spanish and later the United States] to hunt and kill the Tulisane and his men.

Manuelito was at Pasay when news was brought to him that the Macabebes were coming. Instead of running from these fierce little fighters, he decided to meet them, and many people offered to help him, believing that the Anting-Anting would turn away all bullets and give them victory. So Manuelito and many men left the town, built trenches in the hills near San Pedro Macati, and waited for the Macabebes to appear.

They had not long to wait. The Macabebes, hurrying from Manila, reached San Pedro Macati and soon found that Manuelito was waiting to fight them. They left the town at once and advanced on the Tulisane trenches.

It was a great fight. From the other hills close by many people watched the battle. Five times the Macabebes advanced, and were forced to fall back before the fierce fire of the Tulisanes. But the Macabebe never knows defeat, and once more their line went forward and in one terrible charge swept over the trenches and bayoneted the outlaws. In vain Manuelito called on his men to fight. They broke and ran in every direction. Then, seeing that all was lost, Manuelito started to follow them; but a volley rang out, and, struck by twenty bullets, he fell to the ground dead. The Macabebes chased the flying Tulisanes and killed many of the band; only a few men safely reached the mountains.

While the Macabebes were chasing the outlaws, many people came down from the hills and stood around the body of Manuelito. They could hardly believe their eyes, but the many wounds and the blood staining the ground proved that the great Tulisane was indeed dead.

What of the Anting-Anting? Had it lost its power?

One man timidly unbuttoned the shirt of the dead robber and pulled out the charm. The mystery was explained. Fixed firmly in the center of the Anting-Anting was a silver bullet. There was but one explanation. The Macabebes had melted a statue of the Virgin and used it to make bullets to fire at Manuelito. Against such bullets the charm was useless, but against ordinary lead it never would have failed. Had not the people seen Manuelito's own men fire at him?

The charm was taken from the neck of the dead Tulisane and many copies were made of it. Even to this day hundreds of people are wearing them. They will tell you about Manuelito's great fight and also about his famous Anting-Anting.

"But," you say, "the Anting-Anting was useless. Manuelito was killed."

They answer, "Yes, Señor, it is true; but the Macabebes used bullets of silver. Had they used lead the story would have been different. Poor Manuelito!"

Source: "The Anting-Anting of Manuelito," John Maurice Miller. *Philippine Folklore Stories.* (Boston: Ginn, 1904), pp. 33–35.

The Story of Urashima Taro, the Fisher Lad

The following tale is among the most widely remembered traditional narratives among Americans of Japanese descent. In some U.S. variants of the story, the episode of Urashimo Taro's rescue of the tortoise is omitted. A large majority of those who knew the tale claimed that any version that did not include the tortoise rescue would be incomplete, indicating that the importance of being kind to all living things was as significant as the concluding message of obedience to those who are wiser.

Long, long ago in the province of Tango there lived on the shore of Japan in the little fishing village of Mizu-no-ye a young fisherman named Urashima Taro. His father had been a fisherman before him, and his skill had more than doubly descended to his son, for Urashima was the most skillful fisher in all that country side, and could catch more bonito and tai in a day than his comrades could in a week.

But in the little fishing village, more than for being a clever fisher of the sea was he known for his kind heart. In his whole life he had never hurt anything, either great or small, and when a boy, his companions had always laughed at him, for he would never join with them in teasing animals, but always tried to keep them from this cruel sport.

One soft summer twilight he was going home at the end of a day's fishing when he came upon a group of children. They were all screaming and talking at the tops of their voices, and seemed to be in a state of great excitement about something, and on his going up to them to see what was the matter he saw that they were tormenting a tortoise. First one boy pulled it this way, then another boy pulled it that way, while a third child beat it with a stick, and the fourth hammered its shell with a stone.

Now Urashima felt very sorry for the poor tortoise and made up his mind to rescue it. He spoke to the boys: "Look here, boys, you are treating that poor tortoise so badly that it will soon die!"

The boys, who were all of an age when children seem to delight in being cruel to animals, took no notice of Urashima's gentle reproof, but went on teasing it as before. One of the older boys answered: "Who cares whether it lives or dies? We do not. Here, boys, go on, go on!"

And they began to treat the poor tortoise more cruelly than ever. Urashima waited a moment, turning over in his mind what would be the best way to deal with the boys. He would try to persuade them to give the tortoise up to him, so he smiled at them and said: " I am sure you are all good, kind boys! Now won't you give me the tortoise? I should like to have it so much!"

"No, we won't give you the tortoise," said one of the boys. "Why should we? We caught it ourselves."

"What you say is true," said Urashima, "but I do not ask you to give it to me for nothing. I will give you some money for it; in other words, the Ojisan (Uncle) will buy it of you. Won't that do for you, my boys?" He held up the money to them, strung on a piece of string through a hole in the center of each coin. "Look, boys, you can buy anything you like with this money. You can do much more with this money than you can with that poor tortoise. See what good boys you are to listen to me."

The boys were not bad boys at all, they were only mischievous, and as Urashima spoke they were won by his kind smile and gentle words and began "to be of his spirit," as they say in Japan. Gradually they all came up to him, the ringleader of the little band holding out the tortoise to him.

"Very well, Ojisan, we will give you the tortoise if you will give us the money!" And Urashima took the tortoise and gave the money to the boys, who, calling to each other, scampered away and were soon out of sight.

Then Urashima stroked the tortoise's back, saying as he did so: "Oh, you poor thing! Poor thing! there, there! you are safe now! They say that a stork lives for a thousand years, but the tortoise for ten thousand years. You have the longest life of any creature in this world, and you were in great danger of having that precious life cut short by those cruel boys. Luckily I was passing by and saved you, and so life is still yours. Now I am going to take you back to your home, the sea, at once. Do not let yourself be caught again, for there might be no one to save you next time!"

All the time that the kind fisherman was speaking he was walking quickly to the shore and out upon the rocks; then putting the tortoise into the water he watched the animal disappear, and turned homewards himself, for he was tired and the sun had set.

The next morning Urashima went out as usual in his boat. The weather was fine and the sea and sky were both blue and soft in the tender haze of the summer morning. Urashima got into his boat and dreamily pushed out to sea, throwing his line as he did so. He soon passed the other fishing boats and left them behind him till they were lost to sight in the distance, and his boat drifted further and further out upon the blue waters. Somehow, he knew not why, he felt unusually happy that morning; and he could not help wishing that, like the tortoise he set free the day before, he had thousands of years to live instead of his own short span of human life.

He was suddenly startled from his reverie by hearing his own name called: "Urashima, Urashima!" Clear as a bell and soft as the summer wind the name floated over the sea. He stood up and looked in every direction thinking that one of the other boats had overtaken him, but gaze as he might over the wide expanse of water, near or far there was no sign of a boat, so the voice could not have come from any human being.

Startled, and wondering who or what it was that had called him so clearly, he looked in all directions round about him and saw that without his knowing it a tortoise had come to the side of the boat. Urashima saw with surprise that it was the very tortoise he had rescued the day before.

"Well, Mr. Tortoise," said Urashima, "was it you who called my name just now?"

The tortoise nodded its head several times and said: "Yes, it was I. Yesterday in your honorable shadow (o kage sama de) my life was saved, and I have come to offer you my thanks and to tell you how grateful I am for your kindness to me."

"Indeed," said Urashima, "that is very polite of you. Come up into the boat. I would offer you a smoke, but as you are a tortoise doubtless you do not smoke" and the fisherman laughed at the joke.

"He he he he!" laughed the tortoise; "sake (rice wine) is my favorite refreshment, but I do not care for tobacco."

"Indeed," said Urashima, "I regret very much that I have no 'sake' in my boat to offer you, but come up and dry your back in the sun; tortoises always love to do that."

So the tortoise climbed into the boat, the fisherman helping him, and after an exchange of complimentary speeches the tortoise said: "Have you ever seen Rin Gin, the Palace of the Dragon King of the Sea, Urashima?"

The fisherman shook his head and replied, "No; year after year the sea has been my home, but though I have often heard of the Dragon King's realm under the sea I have never yet set eyes on that wonderful place. It must be very far away, if it exists at all!"

"Is that really so? You have never seen the Sea King's Palace? Then you have missed seeing one of the most wonderful sights in the whole universe. It is far away at the bottom of the sea, but if I take you there we shall soon reach the place. If you would like to see the Sea King's land I will be your guide."

"I should like to go there, certainly, and you are very kind to think of taking me, but you must remember that I am only a poor mortal and have not the power of swimming like a sea creature such as you are."

Before the fisherman could say more the tortoise stopped him, saying: "What? You need not swim yourself. If you will ride on my back I will take you without any trouble on your part."

"But," said Urashima, "how is it possible for me to ride on your small back?"

"It may seem absurd to you, but I assure you that you can do so. Try at once! Just come and get on my back, and see if it is as impossible as you think!"

As the tortoise finished speaking, Urashima looked at its shell, and strange to say he saw that the creature had suddenly grown so big that a man could easily sit on its back.

"This is strange indeed!" said Urashima; "then, Mr. Tortoise, with your kind permission I will get on your back. Dokoisho!" he exclaimed as he jumped on.

The tortoise, with an unmoved face, as if this strange proceeding were quite an ordinary event, said: "Now we will set out at our leisure," and with these words he leapt into the sea with Urashima on his back. Down through the water the tortoise dived. For a long time these two strange companions rode through the sea. Urashima never grew tired, nor his clothes moist with the water. At last, far away in the distance a magnificent gate appeared, and behind the gate, the long, sloping roofs of a palace on the horizon.

"Ya," exclaimed Urashima, "that looks like the gate of some large palace just appearing! Mr. Tortoise, can you tell what that place is we can now see?"

"That is the great gate of the Rin Gin Palace. The large roof that you see behind the gate is the Sea King's Palace itself."

"All right."

"Then we have at last come to the realm of the Sea King and to his Palace," said Urashima.

"Yes, indeed," answered the tortoise, "and don't you think we have come very quickly?" And while he was speaking the tortoise reached the side of the gate. "And here we are, and you must please walk from here."

The tortoise now went in front, and speaking to the gatekeeper, said: "This is Urashima Taro, from the country of Japan. I have had the honor of bringing him as a visitor to this kingdom. Please show him the way."

Then the gatekeeper, who was a fish, at once led the way through the gate before them.

The red bream, the flounder, the sole, the cuttlefish, and all the chief vassals of the Dragon King of the Sea now came out with courtly bows to welcome the stranger.

"Urashima Sama, Urashima Sama! Welcome to the Sea Palace, the home of the Dragon King of the Sea. Thrice welcome are you, having come from such a distant country. And you, Mr. Tortoise, we are greatly indebted to you for all your trouble in bringing Urashima here." Then, turning again to Urashima, they said, "Please follow us this way," and from here the whole band of fishes became his guides.

Urashima, being only a poor fisher lad, did not know how to behave in a palace; but, strange though it was all to him, he did not feel ashamed or embarrassed, but followed his kind guides quite calmly where they led to the inner palace.

When he reached the portals a beautiful Princess with her attendant maidens came out to welcome him. She was more beautiful than any human being, and was robed in flowing garments of red and soft green like the under side of a wave, and golden threads glimmered through the folds of her gown. Her lovely black hair streamed over her shoulders in the fashion of a king's daughter many hundreds of years ago, and when she spoke her voice sounded like music over the water.

Urashima was lost in wonder while he looked upon her, and he could not speak. Then he remembered that he ought to bow, but before he could make a low obeisance the Princess took him by the hand and led him to a beautiful hall, and to the seat of honor at the upper end, and bade him be seated.

"Urashima Taro, it gives me the highest pleasure to welcome you to my father's kingdom," said the Princess. "Yesterday you set free a tortoise, and I have sent for you to thank you for saving my life, for I was that tortoise. Now if you like you shall live here forever in the land of eternal youth, where summer never dies and where sorrow never comes, and I will be your bride if you will, and we will live together happily forever afterwards!"

And as Urashima listened to her sweet words and gazed upon her lovely face his heart was filled with a great wonder and joy, and he answered her, wondering if it was not all a dream, "Thank you a thousand times for your kind speech. There is nothing I could wish for more than to he permitted to stay here with you in this beautiful land, of which I have often heard, but have never seen to this day. Beyond all words, this is the most wonderful place I have ever seen."

While he was speaking a train of fishes appeared, all dressed in ceremonial, trailing garments. One by one, silently and with stately steps, they entered the hall, bearing on coral trays delicacies of fish and seaweed, such as no one can dream of, and this wondrous feast was set before the bride and bridegroom. The bridal was celebrated with dazzling splendor, and in the Sea King's realm there was great rejoicing. As soon as the young pair had pledged themselves in the wedding cup of wine, three times three, music was played, and songs were sung, and fishes with silver scales and golden tails stepped in from the waves and danced. Urashima enjoyed himself with all his heart. Never in his whole life had he sat down to such a marvelous feast.

When the feast was over the Princess asked the bridegroom if he would like to walk through the palace and see all there was to be seen. Then the happy fisherman, following his bride, the Sea King's daughter, was shown all the wonders of that enchanted land where youth and joy go hand in hand and neither time nor age can touch them. The palace was built of coral and adorned with pearls, and the beauties and wonders of the place were so great that the tongue fails to describe them.

But, to Urashima, more wonderful than the palace was the garden that surrounded it. Here was to be seen at one time the scenery of the four different seasons; the beauties of summer and winter, spring and autumn, were displayed to the wondering visitor at once.

First, when he looked to the east, the plum and cherry trees were seen in full bloom, the nightingales sang in the pink avenues, and butterflies flitted from flower to flower. Looking to the south all the trees were green in the fullness of summer, and the day cicada and the night cricket chirruped loudly. Looking to the west the autumn maples were ablaze like a sunset sky, and the chrysanthemums were in perfection. Looking to the north the change made Urashima start, for the ground was silver white with snow, and trees and bamboos were also covered with snow and the pond was thick with ice.

And each day there were new joys and new wonders for Urashima, and so great was his happiness that he forgot everything, even the home he had left behind and his parents and his own country, and three days passed without his even thinking of all he had left behind. Then his mind came back to him and he remembered who he was, and that he did not belong to this wonderful land or the Sea King's palace, and he said to himself: "Dear! I must not stay on here, for I have an old father and mother at home. What can have happened to them all this time? How anxious they must have been these days when I did not return as usual. I must go back at once without letting one more day pass." And he began to prepare for the journey in great haste.

Then he went to his beautiful wife, the Princess, and bowing low before her he said: "Indeed, I have been very happy with you for a long time, Otohime Sama" (for that was her name), "and you have been kinder to me than any words can tell. But now I must say good-by. I must go back to my old parents."

Then Otohime Sama began to weep, and said softly and sadly, "Is it not well with you here, Urashima, that you wish to leave me so soon? Where is the haste? Stay with me yet another day only!"

But Urashima had remembered his old parents, and in Japan the duty to parents is stronger than everything else, stronger even than pleasure or love, and he would not be persuaded, but answered, "Indeed, I must go. Do not think that I wish to leave you. It is not that. I must go and see my old parents. Let me go for one day and I will come back to you."

"Then," said the Princess sorrowfully, "there is nothing to be done. I will send you back today to your father and mother, and instead of trying to keep you with me one more day, I shall give you this as a token of our love; please take it back with you;" and she brought him a beautiful lacquer box tied about with a silken cord and tassels of red silk.

Urashima had received so much from the Princess already that he felt some compunction in taking the gift, and said: "It does not seem right for me to take yet another gift from you after all the many favors I have received at your hands, but because it is your wish I will do so," and then he added, "Tell me what is this box?"

"That," answered the Princess "is the TamateBako (Box of the Jewel Hand), and it contains something very precious. You must not open this box, whatever happens! If you open it something dreadful will happen to you! Now promise me that you will never open this box!"

And Urashima promised that he would never, never open the box whatever happened. Then bidding good-by to Otohime Sama he went down to the seashore, the Princess and her attendants following him, and there he found a large tortoise waiting for him.

He quickly mounted the creature's back and was carried away over the shining sea into the East. He looked back to wave his hand to Otohime Sama till at last he could see her no more, and the land of the Sea King and the roofs of the wonderful palace were lost in the far, far distance. Then, with his face turned eagerly towards his own land, he looked for the rising of the blue hills on the horizon before him.

At last the tortoise carried him into the bay he knew so well, and to the shore from whence he had set out. He stepped on to the shore and looked about him while the tortoise rode away back to the Sea King's realm.

But what is the strange fear that seizes Urashima as he stands and looks about him? Why does he gaze so fixedly at the people that pass him by, and why do they in turn stand and look at him?

The shore is the same and the hills are the same, but the people that he sees walking past him have very different faces to those he had known so well before.

Wondering what it can mean he walks quickly towards his old home. Even that looks different, but a house stands on the spot, and he calls out: "Father, I have just returned!" and he was about to enter, when he saw a strange man coming out.

"Perhaps my parents have moved while I have been away, and have gone somewhere else," was the fisherman's thought. Somehow he began to feel strangely anxious, he could not tell why.

"Excuse me," said he to the man who was staring at him, "but till within the last few days I have lived in this house. My name is Urashima Taro. Where have my parents gone whom I left here?"

A very bewildered expression came over the face of the man, and, still gazing intently on Urashima's face, he said: "What? Are you Urashima Taro?"

"Yes," said the fisherman, "I am Urashima Taro!"

"Ha, ha!" laughed the man, "you must not make such jokes. It is true that once upon a time a man called Urashima Taro did live in this village, but that is a story three hundred years old. He could not possibly be alive now!"

When Urashima heard these strange words he was frightened, and said: "Please, please, you must not joke with me, I am greatly perplexed. I am really Urashima Taro, and I certainly have not lived three hundred years. Till four or five days ago I lived on this spot. Tell me what I want to know without more joking, please."

But the man's face grew more and more grave, and he answered: "You may or may not be Urashima Taro, I don't know. But the Urashima Taro of whom I have heard is a man who lived three hundred years ago. Perhaps you are his spirit come to revisit your old home?"

"Why do you mock me?" said Urashima. "I am no spirit! I am a living man; do you not see my feet"; and "don-don" he stamped on the ground, first with one foot and then with the other to show the man. (Japanese ghosts have no feet.)

"But Urashima Taro lived three hundred years ago, that is all I know; it is written in the village chronicles," persisted the man, who could not believe what the fisherman said.

Urashima was lost in bewilderment and trouble. He stood looking all around him, terribly puzzled, and, indeed, something in the appearance of everything was different to what he remembered before he went away, and the awful feeling came over him that what the man said was perhaps true. He seemed to be in a strange dream. The few days he had spent in the Sea King's palace beyond the sea had not been days at all; they had been hundreds of years, and in that time his parents had died and all the people he had ever known, and the village had written down his story. There was no use in staying here any longer. He must get back to his beautiful wife beyond the sea.

He made his way back to the beach, carrying in his hand the box which the Princess had given him. But which was the way? He could not find it alone! Suddenly he remembered the box, the TamateBako.

"The Princess told me when she gave me the box never to open it, that it contained a very precious thing. But now that I have no home, now that I have lost everything that was dear to me here, and my heart grows thin with sadness, at such a time, if I open the box, surely I shall find something that will help me, something that will show me the way back to my beautiful Princess over the sea. There is nothing else for me to do now. Yes, yes, I will open the box and look in!"

And so his heart consented to this act of disobedience, and he tried to persuade himself that he was doing the right thing in breaking his promise.

Slowly, very slowly, he untied the red silk cord, slowly and wonderingly he lifted the lid of the precious box. And what did he find? Strange to say only a beautiful little purple cloud rose out of the box in three soft wisps. For an instant it covered his face and wavered over him as if loath to go, and then it floated away like vapor over the sea.

Urashima, who had been till that moment like a strong and handsome youth of twenty-four, suddenly became very, very old. His back doubled up with age, his hair turned snowy white, his face wrinkled and he fell down dead on the beach.

Poor Urashima! Because of his disobedience he could never return to the Sea King's realm or the lovely Princess beyond the sea.

Little children, never be disobedient to those who are wiser than you, for disobedience was the beginning of all the miseries and sorrows of life.

Source: "The Story of Urashima Taro, the Fisher Lad," Yei Theodora Ozaki. *Japanese Fairy Tales.* (New York: Grosset and Dunlap, 1906), pp. 24–42.

The Juan Who Visited Heaven

"Juan" is a stock name for male characters in Filipino folktales in both the United States and in many areas of the Philippines. Although Juan is often a comic numskull figure, in this case he is a devout child born in answer to his parents' prayers. At the death of his mother during his birth, the newborn began a career of miraculous acts, becoming the protégé first of the local priest and then of Jesus. The narrative's plot suggests similar plots of precocious European folktale heroes. In this tale as developed among the Christian Filipinos, however, the secular pattern has been transformed to a sacred biography.

There was a couple who had always been childless. No matter how it looked, whether deformed or ugly, they must have a child. So after a short time they saw that their prayers would be answered, and in the course of nature a child was born, but the mother died at the birth. The newborn child ran to the church, climbed into the tower, and began to hammer on the bells. The priest, hearing the noise, sent the sacristan to see what was the matter. The sacristan went, and seeing there a little child, asked what he was doing and told him to stop, for the priest would be angry; but the ringing of the bells went on.

Then the priest went up. "Little boy," he said, "what is your name?"

"Juan," said the child.

"Why are you ringing the church bells?"

"Because my mother is dead."

"When did she die?"

"Only now."

"If you stop ringing the bells she shall have a fine funeral and you shall live with me and be as my son," said the priest.

"Very well, sir, if you will let me stay in the church all I wish." To this the priest assented. The dead woman was buried with all the pomp of music, candles, and bells, and the boy went to live in the convent. Always after his school was done he would be in the church. The father did everything that was possible for him, for he knew that he was not a natural child.

After a time the padre sent for him to get his dinner, but he would not leave the church, so the priest had a good dinner cooked and sent it down to the church, but he told the sacristan to watch the church and see what happened. The sacristan watched and soon saw the statue of Jesus eating with the boy. This he told the padre, and the child's dinner was always sent to the church after that.

One day not long after he went to the priest and said, "Master, my friend down at the church wants me to go away with him."

"Where are you going?"

"My friend wants me to go to heaven with him." The priest consented and the little boy and the Lord Jesus went away together. As they walked the little boy saw that two roads ran along together, one thorny and the other smooth.

Asked the boy of his companion, "Friend, why is this road where we walk so thorny, and that other yonder so smooth?"

Said the Lord, "Hush, child, it is not fitting to disturb the peace of this place, but I will tell you. This is the path of the sinless and is thorny, but that smooth way yonder is the way of the sinners and never reaches heaven."

Again they came to a great house filled with young men and women who were all working hammering iron.

Said the little boy, "Who are those who labor with the hammer?"

"Hush, child, they are the souls of those who died unmarried."

They journeyed on, and on one side were bush pastures filled with poor cattle while on the opposite side of the road were pastures dry and bare where the cattle were very fat. The child inquired the meaning of the mystery.

The Lord answered him, "Hush, child! These lean cattle in the rich pastures are the souls of sinners, while those fat cattle on dry and sunburnt ground are the souls of sinless ones."

After a while they crossed a river, one part of which was ruby red and the other spotless white. "Friend, what is this?" asked the boy.

"Hush, child, the red is the blood of your mother whose life was given for yours, and the white is the milk which she desired to give to you, her child," said the Lord.

At last they came to a great house having seven stories, and there on a table they saw many candles, some long, some short, some burned out. Said Juan, "Friend, what are all these candles?"

"Hush, child, those are the lives of your friends."

"What are those empty candle-sticks?"

"Those are your mother and your uncle, who are dead."

"Who is this long one?"

"That is your father, who has long to live."

"Who is this very short one?"

"That is your master, who will die soon."

"May I put in another?"

"Yes, child, if you wish." So he changed it for a long one, and with his heavenly companion he returned to earth.

There he told his master, the padre, all that he had seen and heard and how he had changed the candles; and he and his master lived together a very long time. And in the fullness of time the padre died, but Juan went to heaven one day with his Lord and never returned.

Source: "The Juan Who Went to Heaven," Fletcher Gardner. "Tagalog Folk-Tales, I." *Journal of American Folklore* 20 (1907): 104–116, pp. 111–112.

Select Bibliography

Choy, Bong-Youn. *Koreans in America*. Chicago: Nelson Hall, 1979.

Claus, Peter J., Sarah Diamond, and Margaret Ann Mills. *South Asian Folklore: An Encyclopedia: Afghanistan, Bangladesh, India, Nepal, Pakistan, Sri Lanka*. London: Taylor & Francis, 2003.

Daniels, Roger. *Asian America: Chinese and Japanese in the United States since 1850*. Seattle: University of Washington Press, 1988.

Korom, Frank J. *South Asian Folklore: A Handbook*. Westport, CT: Greenwood Press, 2006.

Lim, Shirley Geok-Lin, and Amy Ling. *Reading the Literatures of Asian America*. Philadelphia: Temple University Press, 1992.

Meñez, Herminia Quimpo. *Explorations in Philippine Folklore*. Quezon City, Philippines: Ateneo de Manila University Press, 1996.

Opler, Marvin K. "Japanese Folk Beliefs and Practices, Tule Lake, California." *Journal of American Folklore* 63 (1950): 385–397.

Radin, Paul. "Folktales of Japan as Told in California." *Journal of American Folklore* 59 (1946): 289–308.

Takaki, Ronald. *Strangers from a Different Shore: A History of Asian Americans*. Revised edition. Boston: Bay Books, 1998.

Toelken, Barre. "Cultural Maintenance and Ethnic Intensification in Two Japanese American World War II Internment Camps." *Oriens Extremus* 33 (1990): 69–94.

Index

About the Author

THOMAS A. GREEN is Associate Professor of Anthropology at Texas A&M University. His many books include *The Greenwood Library of American Folktales* (2006) and *The Greenwood Library of World Folktales* (2008).